MAUS

PANTHEON BO

AUS

II

A SURVIVOR'S TALE

AND HERE
MY TROUBLES
BEGAN

art spiegelman

OKS NEW YORK

Thanks to Paul Pavel, Deborah Karl, and Mala Spiegelman for helping this volume into the world.

Thanks to the John Simon Guggenheim Memorial Foundation for a fellowship that allowed me to focus on completing Maus.

And my thanks, with love and admiration, to Francoise Mouly for her intelligence, integrity, editorial skills, and for her love.

Chapters one through four were originally published in somewhat different form in Raw magazine between 1986 and 1991.

Library of Congress Cataloging-in-Publication Data
Spiegelman, Art.
Maus: a survivor's tale, II: and here my troubles began/Art Spiegelman.
p.   cm.
ISBN 0-679-72977-1
1. Spiegelman, Vladek — Comic books, strips, etc.
2. Holocaust, Jewish (1939-1945) — Poland — Biography — Comic books, strips, etc.
3. Holocaust survivors — United States — Biography — Comic books, strips, etc.
4. Spiegelman, Art — Comic books, strips, etc.
5. Children of Holocaust survivors — United States — Biography — Comic books, strips, etc. I. Title.
D804.3.S66   1991
940.53'18'0207 — dc20   91-52739

Book design: art spiegelman and Louise Fili

Manufactured in the United States of America

468D975

"Mickey Mouse is the most miserable ideal ever revealed....Healthy emotions tell every independent young man and every honorable youth that the dirty and filth-covered vermin, the greatest bacteria carrier in the animal kingdom, cannot be the ideal type of animal....Away with Jewish brutalization of the people! Down with Mickey Mouse! Wear the Swastika Cross!"

—newspaper article, Pomerania, Germany, mid-1930s

FOR RICHIEU

AND FOR NADJA

ART SPIEGELMAN, a cartoonist born after WW II, is working on a book about what happened to his parents as Jews in wartime Poland. He has made a series of visits to his childhood home in Rego Park, N.Y., to record his father's memories. Art's mother, Anja, committed suicide in 1968. Art becomes furious when he learns that his father, **VLADEK**, has burned Anja's wartime memoirs. Vladek is remarried to Mala, another survivor. She complains often of his stinginess and lack of concern for her. Vladek, a diabetic who has suffered two heart attacks, is in poor health.

In Poland, Vladek had been a small-time textile salesman. In 1937 he married Anja Zylberberg, the youngest daughter of a wealthy Sosnowiec hosiery family. They had a son, Richieu, who died during the war.

Forced first into ghettos, then into hiding, Vladek and Anja tried to escape to Hungary with their prewar acquaintances, the Mandelbaums, whose nephew, Abraham, had attested in a letter that the escape route was safe. They were caught and, in March, 1944, they were brought to the gates of Auschwitz.

AND HERE MY TROUBLES BEGAN
(FROM MAUSCHWITZ TO THE CATSKILLS AND BEYOND)

CONTENTS

HALT!

11

I'VE GOT IT!...PANEL ONE: MY FATHER IS ON HIS EXERCYCLE...

I TELL HIM I JUST MARRIED A FROG...

PANEL TWO: HE FALLS OFF HIS CYCLE IN SHOCK.

SO, YOU AND I GO TO A MOUSE RABBI. HE SAYS A FEW MAGIC WORDS AND ZAP!...

BY THE END OF THE PAGE THE FROG HAS TURNED INTO A BEAUTIFUL MOUSE!

HMPH

I ONLY CONVERTED TO MAKE VLADEK HAPPY.

YEAH. BUT NOTHING CAN MAKE HIM HAPPY.

YOU KNOW, YOU SHOULD HAVE MARRIED WHAT'S-HER-NAME? THE GIRL YOU WERE SEEING WHEN WE FIRST MET?...

SANDRA?

YES. THEN YOU COULD JUST DRAW MICE, NO PROBLEM.

C'MON. I JUST DATED HER TO GET OVER MY PREJUDICE AGAINST MIDDLE-CLASS, NEW YORK, JEWISH WOMEN.

THEY REMIND ME TOO MUCH OF MY RELATIVES TO BE EROTIC, SO I JUST—

ART! FRANÇOISE!!

HURRY—YOUR FATHER JUST PHONED US! HE HAD A HEART ATTACK!

WHAT?

OH NO!

HE LEFT THIS NUMBER TO CALL.

WE JUST SAW HIM LAST WEEK... ON THE WAY UP HERE WE STOPPED AT THEIR BUNGALOW IN THE CATSKILLS... HE LOOKED FINE...

HI, POP... HOW ARE YOU? HOW COME YOU'RE NOT IN A *HOSPITAL*?... HUH?

BUT-? YOU *DIDN'T*? YOU'RE *NOT*?! BUT WHY DID YOU-? *SHE DID*?

BUT *WHEN*?? *WHAT*??? I CAN'T HEAR YOU. SPEAK UP. ...NO,...DON'T CRY, POP...

JEEZIS. I *GUESS* SO... TONIGHT?? I DUNNO. UM... OKAY, OKAY. WE'LL TALK ABOUT IT THEN...

JUST RELAX... OKAY... WILL YOU BE ALRIGHT? YES...I -UM- LOVE YOU TOO. ...SEE YOU SOON...G'BYE...

WHEW.

WHAT IS IT? WHAT HAPPENED??

IS YOUR FATHER OKAY?

HE DIDN'T EVEN *HAVE* A HEART ATTACK... HE JUST WANTED TO BE SURE I'D CALL HIM BACK!

YOU'RE *KIDDING*! HOW COULD HE DO SUCH A THING!

MALA LEFT HIM. SHE TOOK MONEY OUT OF THEIR ACCOUNT AND DROVE OFF. HE WANTS US TO STAY WITH HIM AT HIS BUN- GALOW FOR A WHILE.

I-I GUESS WE HAVE TO GO.

I GUESS SO.

WHAT A PITY. YOU JUST **GOT** UP HERE...

WE'LL BE BACK.

WE'RE NOT TAKING MUCH LUGGAGE, SO WE HAVE AN EXCUSE NOT TO STAY LONG.

VLADEK SOUNDED HALF-HYSTERICAL ON THE PHONE.

POOR GUY...I FEEL SO SORRY FOR HIM.

YEAH, ME TOO... 'TIL I HAVE TO SPEND ANY TIME WITH HIM— THEN HE DRIVES ME **CRAZY!**

MM.

SIGH.

DEPRESSED AGAIN?

JUST THINKING ABOUT MY BOOK... IT'S SO **PRESUMPTUOUS** OF ME.

I MEAN, I CAN'T EVEN MAKE ANY SENSE OUT OF MY RELATIONSHIP WITH MY FATHER... HOW AM I SUPPOSED TO MAKE ANY SENSE OUT OF AUSCHWITZ?...OF THE HOLOCAUST?...

WHEN I WAS A KID I USED TO THINK ABOUT WHICH OF MY PARENTS I'D LET THE NAZIS TAKE TO THE OVENS IF I COULD ONLY SAVE ONE OF THEM...

USUALLY I SAVED MY MOTHER. DO YOU THINK THAT'S NORMAL?

NOBODY'S NORMAL.

I WONDER IF RICHIEU AND I WOULD GET ALONG IF HE WAS STILL ALIVE.

YOUR BROTHER?

MY *GHOST*-BROTHER, SINCE HE GOT KILLED BEFORE I WAS BORN. HE WAS ONLY FIVE OR SIX.

AFTER THE WAR MY PARENTS TRACED DOWN THE VAGUEST RUMORS, AND WENT TO ORPHANAGES ALL OVER EUROPE. THEY COULDN'T BELIEVE HE WAS DEAD.

I DIDN'T THINK ABOUT HIM MUCH WHEN I WAS GROWING UP... HE WAS MAINLY A LARGE, BLURRY PHOTOGRAPH HANGING IN MY PARENTS' BEDROOM.

UH-HUH. I THOUGHT THAT WAS A PICTURE OF YOU, THOUGH IT DIDN'T *LOOK* LIKE YOU.

THAT'S THE POINT. THEY DIDN'T *NEED* PHOTOS OF ME IN THEIR ROOM... I WAS *ALIVE*!...

THE PHOTO NEVER THREW TANTRUMS OR GOT IN ANY KIND OF TROUBLE.... IT WAS AN IDEAL KID, AND I WAS A PAIN IN THE ASS. I COULDN'T COMPETE.

THEY DIDN'T *TALK* ABOUT RICHIEU, BUT THAT PHOTO WAS A KIND OF REPROACH. HE'D HAVE BECOME A *DOCTOR*, AND MARRIED A WEALTHY JEWISH GIRL...THE CREEP.

BUT AT LEAST WE COULD'VE MADE *HIM* GO DEAL WITH VLADEK. ...IT'S *SPOOKY*, HAVING SIBLING RIVALRY WITH A SNAPSHOT!

I NEVER FELT **GUILTY** ABOUT RICHIEU. BUT I DID HAVE NIGHTMARES ABOUT S.S. MEN COMING INTO MY CLASS AND DRAGGING ALL US JEWISH KIDS AWAY.

DON'T GET ME WRONG. I WASN'T **OBSESSED** WITH THIS STUFF ... IT'S JUST THAT SOMETIMES I'D FANTASIZE ZYKLON B COMING OUT OF OUR SHOWER INSTEAD OF WATER.

I KNOW THIS IS INSANE, BUT I SOMEHOW WISH I HAD BEEN IN AUSCHWITZ **WITH** MY PARENTS SO I COULD REALLY KNOW WHAT THEY LIVED THROUGH!

...I GUESS IT'S **SOME** KIND OF GUILT ABOUT HAVING HAD AN EASIER LIFE THAN THEY DID.

SIGH. I FEEL SO INADEQUATE TRYING TO RECONSTRUCT A REALITY THAT WAS WORSE THAN MY DARKEST DREAMS.

AND TRYING TO DO IT AS A **COMIC STRIP!** I GUESS I BIT OFF MORE THAN I CAN CHEW. MAYBE I OUGHT TO FORGET THE WHOLE THING.

THERE'S SO MUCH I'LL NEVER BE ABLE TO UNDERSTAND OR VISUALIZE. I MEAN, REALITY IS TOO **COMPLEX** FOR COMICS... SO MUCH HAS TO BE LEFT OUT OR DISTORTED.

JUST KEEP IT HONEST, HONEY.

SEE WHAT I MEAN... IN REAL LIFE YOU'D **NEVER** HAVE LET ME TALK THIS LONG WITHOUT INTERRUPTING.

HMMPH. LIGHT ME A CIGARETTE.

And so, the Catskills...

HE SAID HE'D LEAVE THE KEY ABOVE THE-AH. THERE IT IS!

COSMOPOLITAN BUNGALOWS

ARTIE?

YAWN. SO, DARLINGS— YOU **CAME** FINALLY. I WAITED AND I WAITED AND I COULDN'T SLEEP.

EMERGENCY OXYGEN UNIT.

YOU SEE HOW IT IS NOW, ARTIE. SHE TOOK MY MONEY AND SHE RAN AWAY. **OY!** HOW COULD SHE DO IT, TO LEAVE SUCH A SICK MAN LIKE ME ALONE??

BUT NOW, AT LEAST, I'M HAPPY I HAVE HERE YOU "KIDS" TO STAY TOGETHER WITH ME...

LOOK HOW NICE I MADE FOR YOU A BED. FOR THE WHOLE **SUMMER** YOU CAN BE COMFORTABLE HERE!

HEY! WE'RE JUST STAYING FOR A FEW DAYS, POP. WE—

WELL! IN THE MORNING WE CAN SPEAK MORE—BUT NOW YOU CAN MAKE YOUR-SELF AT HOME, SO AS LIKE IT'S YOUR OWN.

G'NIGHT, POP.

(MY GOD—DOES HE EXPECT US TO STAY HERE ALL SUMMER?)

(I GUESS SO. IF HE HAD HIS WAY WE'D MOVE TO **QUEENS** WITH HIM TOO. HE—)

PLEASE! I'M SO TIRED FROM WAITING 'TIL YOU CAME. **TOMORROW** YOU CAN TALK!

SUCH A SUNNY DAY AND **STILL** YOU'RE BOTH SLEEPING?!

WHU? WHATIME IZZIT?

IT'S ALMOST 8:00, AND ALREADY I'VE MADE FOR A HALF HOUR ON THE PORCH MY GYMNASTICS. SINCE I WAS A **BOY** I'VE MADE EVERY DAY MY EXERCISES...

UNH?

AT FIRST THE NEIGHBORS TRIED TO MAKE EXERCISES **WITH** ME, BUT THEY COULDN'T KEEP UP... SO NOW ONLY THEY WATCH!

IS THERE ANY COFFEE?

MALA HAD HERE SOME **INSTANT** COFFEE... TOMORROW WE'LL EXERCISE **TOGETHER.**

WHA? **MY** ONLY EXERCISE IS WALKING OUT FOR CIGARETTES! ...INSTANT COFFEE'LL HAVE TO DO.

YOU HAVE TO HURRY NOW TO GET READY... TODAY I NEED YOU'LL HELP ME TO PREPARE MY BANK AND TAX PAPERS- MALA LEFT THEM IN A MESS, YOU CAN'T IMAGINE!

?

YAH-HERE I HAVE IT. IT'S THE CAFFEINE-FREE KIND OF COFFEE.

GROAN.

UM. HAVE YOU SEEN MY **PANTS**?

ALL YOUR THINGS I PUT ALREADY IN ORDER IN THE BUREAU, THERE.

WELL... THANKS FOR NOT THROW-ING THEM OUT.

WAKE UP, HONEY. I'VE GOT BAD NEWS. THE ONLY COFFEE HERE IS **SANKA**!

UNF? I BROUGHT **OUR** COFFEE AND OUR POT. LOOK IN MY BAG.

ACH!

NOW WHAT? — I'M MAKING FOR YOU *BREAKFAST*, AND I SEE HERE THE *SALT!* JUST *LOOK* WHAT MALA DID...

THE SALT HERE, IT'S HALF *FULL*, AND SHE OPENED *ANYWAY* A NEW ONE!

I CAN'T EAT ON MY DIET *ANY* SODIUM. I DON'T NEED EVEN *ONE* CONTAINER SALT, AND HERE IT'S *TWO* OPEN SALTS!

SO...WHAT HAPPENED? WHY DID MALA LEAVE?

SHE WANTS THAT ALL MY MONEY, WHAT I WORKED SO HARD ALL MY LIFE, IT WILL ONLY BE FOR HER.

I HAD A DOCTOR'S APPOINTMENT IN REGO PARK AND WE WENT AFTER TO THE BANK TO RENEW SOME BONDS.

ONE I WANTED IN TRUST OF MALA, ONE FOR MY BROTHER IN ISRAEL, AND ONE I WANTED FOR *YOU*...

BUT SHE DIDN'T LIKE I'LL PUT FOR YOU AND PINEK ANYTHING—SHE SCREAMED LIKE A *CRAZY* PERSON!

SHE DROVE AWAY AND LEFT ME BY THE BANK, AND WHEN I WALKED HOME SHE WAS GONE ALREADY.

THE LAWYER SAYS I MUST MAKE *DRASTIC* STEPS. SHE STOLE AWAY THE JEWELRY, THE CAR AND THE CASH OUT FROM OUR JOINT ACCOUNT—I CAN MAKE *CHARGES!*

OH, C'MON...

19

WHERE'S MALA NOW?

TO FLORIDA SHE DROVE. WE'RE BUYING THERE A CONDO. SHE WANTS TO SELL AND TO GRAB OUT THE DEPOSIT MONEY.

BUT THIS SHE CAN'T DO. SHE NEEDS MY SIG— ARTIE! WHAT DO YOU DO?!!

HUH? I'M JUST LIGHTING MY CIGARETTE...

BETTER YOU SHOULDN'T SMOKE: FOR YOU IT'S TERRIBLE, AND FOR ME, WITH MY SHORTNESS OF BREATH, IT'S ALSO NO GOOD TO BE NEAR...

BUT IF ANYWAY YOU'RE SMOKING, PLEASE DON'T USE FROM ME MY WOODEN MATCHES. I DON'T HAVE LEFT SO MANY, AND ALREADY TO MAKE COFFEE YOU USED ONE.

ONLY TO LIGHT THE OVEN I USE THEM. THESE WOOD MATCHES I HAVE TO BUY! THE PAPER MATCHES I CAN HAVE FREE FROM THE LOBBY OF THE PINES HOTEL.

JEEZ! I'LL BUY YOU A WHOLE BOX OF WOODEN MATCHES!

IT ISN'T NECESSARY... AT HOME OUR OVEN IS AUTOMATIC, AND HERE I'M STAYING ONLY 15 MORE DAYS.

AND I HAVE STILL 50 MATCHES LEFT. HOW MANY MATCHES CAN I USE?...

WHAT A MISER! I CAN'T TAKE ANY MORE. I'M GOING OUT FOR AIR!

ALWAYS ARTIE IS NERVOUS—SO LIKE HIS MOTHER—SHE ALSO WAS NERVOUS.

BAH.

PSST.

YOU MUST BE ARTIE. I'M MRS. KARP. WE'RE NEIGHBORS.

YES. MY DAD MENTIONED THAT YOU'VE LOOKED AFTER HIM WHILE MALA'S GONE.

HE SAID *THAT*? WELL...EDGAR *DID* GIVE HIM A RIDE BACK HERE A FEW DAYS AGO. MALA HAS THEIR CAR NOW, BUT—**COME**, VISIT A MINUTE!

HUH? I CAN'T! I—UH—

LOOK, EDDIE. LOOK WHAT I FOUND: VLADEK'S BOY, ARTIE!

SO! YOU CAME TO TAKE YOUR FATHER TO LIVE BY YOU?

WHAT? NO, WE'RE JUST HELPING HIM GET HIS BEARINGS FOR A FEW DAYS. HE'LL STAY UP HERE 'TIL LABOR DAY.

WHAT? ALONE? HOW CAN HE MANAGE?

HE CAN GET BY. BUT IT'D BE NICE IF YOU GAVE HIM RIDES TO TOWN...LOOKED IN ON HIM SOMETIMES...

MAYBE SOMETIMES, BUT HE'S A SICK OLD MAN. HE CAN'T BE ALL ALONE...

AND **AFTER** THE SUMMER? THEN HE'LL GO LIVE BY YOU, OR WHAT?

NO! I DUNNO WHAT HE'LL DO. MAYBE HE'LL NEED A NURSE OR SOMETHING.

A NURSE, IT COSTS **MONEY**. YOU THINK YOUR FATHER SPENDS MONEY SO EASY?

POOR MALA. ONE TIME I WENT TO THE **SUPERMARKET** WITH HER...

SHE HAD TO ERASE A **HAIRBRUSH** FROM THE BILL BECAUSE HE WOULDN'T PAY FOR HER *PERSONAL* ITEMS—HOW COULD A COUPLE LIVE LIKE THAT?

ART? HELLO? WHERE ARE YOU HONEY?

21

MY WIFE IS CALL-ING ME... YOUR WIFE, SHE'S **JEWISH**?

(HUSH ED-GAR!) INVITE HER IN FOR LEMONADE. MAYBE SOME OTHER TIME. I'D BETTER GO NOW...

WHEW. SO **THERE** YOU ARE !...

WHERE **WERE** YOU? A COUPLE OF VLADEK'S FRIENDS, THE KARPS, JUST HIJACKED ME... Y'KNOW EVEN **THEY** CAN'T STAND HIM.

IT'S SO **CLAUSTROPHOBIC** BEING AROUND VLADEK. HE STRAIGHTENS EVERYTHING YOU TOUCH—HE'S SO **ANXIOUS.** HE NEVER LEARNED HOW TO RELAX.

MAYBE AUSCHWITZ MADE HIM LIKE THAT. MAYBE. BUT LOTS OF THE PEOPLE UP HERE ARE SURVIVORS—LIKE THOSE KARPS—IF THEY'RE WHACKED UP IT'S IN A **DIFFERENT** WAY FROM VLADEK.

OH, ABOUT VLADEK'S MATCHES—IT'S EVEN CRAZIER THAN YOU THOUGHT...

SINCE GAS IS INCLUDED IN THE RENT, HE LEAVES A BURNER LIT ALL DAY TO SAVE ON MATCHES.

GOD, IF IT WASN'T SO PATHETIC, IT'D BE KINDA **FUNNY.** **SO!** YOU'VE BEEN ENJOYING YOURSELF, KIDS? COME—WE'LL SIT TOGETHER AND YOU CAN HELP ME TO PREPARE MY BANK PAPERS.

WHAT ARE YOUR PLANS NOW, POP?

WE'LL WALK OVER TO THE PINES HOTEL AND THEN BACK

I MEAN, IN GENERAL, NOW THAT MALA IS GONE.

MAYBE WE'LL TOGETHER STAY TO THE END OF THE SUMMER HERE...

IT'S SO BEAUTIFUL...

I TOLD YOU-FRANÇOISE AND I CAN ONLY STAY THROUGH THE WEEKEND.

SO? THEN WHEN YOU GO BACK, I ALSO WILL GO. WHAT HAVE I HERE TO STAY ALL ALONE?

AND THEN?

NU? MAYBE YOU'LL WANT WITH ME IN QUEENS TO STAY?

TO HAVE YOU WITH ME, IT'S ALWAYS A PLEASURE. ...REMEMBER, MY HOUSE IT'S ALSO YOUR HOUSE TOO.

I'M SORRY, POP. I DON'T THINK IT WOULD WORK OUT. I MEAN, WE'VE GOT OUR OWN PLACE TO LIVE, AND-

YES. YOU DON'T HAVE TO ANSWER NOW... ONLY TO THINK OF IT...

UM-CAN I ASK YOU MORE ABOUT YOUR PAST... ABOUT AUSCHWITZ?

OF COURSE, DARLING. TO ME YOU CAN ASK ANYTHING!

WELL...WHAT HAPPENED WHEN YOU AND MOM ARRIVED THERE AND WERE SEPARATED?

WHEN WE CAME, THEY PUSHED IN ONE WAY THE MEN, AND SOMEWHERE ELSE THE WOMEN.

OUT!

I WAVED VERY FAST GOODBYE TO ANJA.

24

BUT YOU UNDERSTAND, **NEVER** ANJA AND I WERE SEPARATED!

NO??

NO! THE WAR PUT US APART. BUT ALWAYS, BEFORE AND AFTER, WE WERE TOGETHER.

NOT SO LIKE MALA, WHAT GRABS OUT MY MONEY!—

AUSCHWITZ, POP. TELL ME ABOUT AUSCHWITZ.

AUSCHWITZ WAS IN A TOWN CALLED OSWIECIM. BEFORE THE WAR I CAME OFTEN HERE TO SELL MY TEXTILES.

...AND NOW, I CAME AGAIN.

WE CAME TO A BIG HALL AND THEY SHOUTED ON US.

GET UNDRESSED! LEAVE YOUR VALUABLES! LINE UP! SCHNELL!

I WAS, AT THAT TIME, STILL WITH MY FRIEND MANDELBAUM.

THEY TOOK FROM US OUR PAPERS, OUR CLOTHES AND OUR HAIR—

(PSST— WH-WHAT'S GOING TO HAPPEN TO US?)

(DON'T WORRY.)

WE WERE COLD, AND WE WERE AFRAID.

(IF THEY BROUGHT YOU HERE, THEY'LL PUT YOU TO WORK. THEY'RE NOT READY TO KILL YOU YET.)

(WHAT ABOUT OUR WIVES AND OUR—)

SHUT UP, YIDS! TO THE BATH HOUSE. QUICK!

EVERYWHERE WE HAD TO RUN—SO LIKE *JOGGERS*— AND THEY RAN US TO THE SAUNA...

IT'S FREEZING!

JUST THANK GOD IT'S NOT GAS!

HERE IT WAS THE **LIVE** SHOWERS, NOT THE DEAD GAS SHOWERS WHAT WE HEARD SOMETIMES RUMORS.

IN THE SNOW THEY THREW TO US PRISONERS CLOTHINGS.

ONE GUY TRIED TO EXCHANGE.

SCHNELL! SCHNELL! SCHNELL!

THEY NEVER EVEN *LOOKED* ON WHAT SIZE THEY THREW.

E-EXCUSE ME. THESE SHOES ARE TOO SMALL.

MAYBE **NOW** THEY'LL FIT!

CRAK

THE SHOES WERE **WOOD** SHOES!

I WAS A LUCKY ONE. EVERYTHING FITTED ME A LITTLE. ONLY THE SHIRT WAS TORN AND TOO BIG FOR ME ...

THEY REGISTERED US IN... THEY TOOK FROM US OUR NAMES. AND HERE THEY PUT ME MY NUMBER.

175113

ALL AROUND WAS A SMELL SO TERRIBLE, I CAN'T EXPLAIN... SWEETISH... SO LIKE RUBBER BURNING. AND **FAT.**

HERE WAS **ABRAHAM** — MANDELBAUM'S NEPHEW!

UNCLE! UNCLE!

WHEN WE CAME INSIDE THE GATES SOMEONE RAN TO US FROM FAR AWAY.

SO, UNCLE... YOU'VE ENDED UP HERE TOO.

YOU **TOLD** US TO COME!

YOU WROTE US ABOUT HOW **HAPPY** YOU ARE IN HUNGARY - THAT WE SHOULD JOIN YOU RIGHT AWAY! WELL... HERE WE ARE.

HUN-GARY. HAH!

THE POLES WHO ARRANGED OUR "ESCAPE" UNDERSTOOD **YIDDISH.** SO THEY KNEW YOU WERE WAITING TO HEAR IF I WAS SAFE.

IN BIELSKO THE POLES DICTATED THAT LETTER WHILE THE GESTAPO HELD A PISTOL UP TO MY HEAD.

WHAT COULD I DO? THEY'D HAVE SHOT ME THEN AND THERE.

WELL... SO HERE'S OUR HUNGARY...

AND THERE'S ONLY ONE WAY OUT OF HERE FOR ALL OF US ... THROUGH THOSE CHIMNEYS.

ABRAHAM I DIDN'T SEE AGAIN.... I THINK HE CAME OUT THE CHIMNEY.

BUT I SAW AGAIN ONCE THE POLES WHO BETRAYED US.

THE GERMANS DIDN'T NEED THEM. SO THEY FINISHED ALSO IN AUSCHWITZ.

WE NEWCOMERS WERE PUT INSIDE A ROOM. OLD-TIMERS PASSED AND SAID ALL THE SAME.

I WAS WORN AND SHIVERING AND CRYING A LITTLE.

BUT FROM ANOTHER ROOM SOMEONE APPROACHED OVER

YOU SEE THOSE CHIMNEYS?...

OKAY. SO I WAS **MORE** SAD.

NOBODY EVEN **LOOKED.**

WHY ARE YOU CRYING, MY SON?

SHOULD I BE **HAPPY?** AM I AT A CARNIVAL?

LET ME SEE YOUR ARM...

HE WAS A PRIEST...

HMM... YOUR NUMBER STARTS WITH 17. IN HEBREW THAT'S "K'MINYAN TOV." SEVENTEEN IS A VERY GOOD OMEN...

HE WASN'T JEWISH — BUT VERY INTELLIGENT!

IT ENDS WITH 13, THE AGE A JEWISH BOY BECOMES A MAN...

AND **LOOK!** ADDED TOGETHER IT TOTALS 18. THAT'S "CHAI," THE HEBREW NUMBER OF LIFE.

I CAN'T KNOW IF **I'LL** SURVIVE THIS HELL, BUT I'M CERTAIN **YOU'LL** COME THROUGH ALL THIS ALIVE!

I STARTED TO BELIEVE. I TELL YOU, HE PUT ANOTHER LIFE IN ME.

AND WHENEVER IT WAS VERY BAD I LOOKED AND SAID: "YES. THE PRIEST WAS **RIGHT!** IT TOTALS EIGHTEEN.

WHEW, THAT GUY WAS A **SAINT!**

YES... I NEVER SAW HIM AGAIN.

FOR ME IT WAS HARD HERE, BUT FOR MY FRIEND MANDELBAUM IT WAS **MORE** HARD.

IN SOSNOWIEC, EVERYONE KNEW MANDELBAUM. HE WAS OLDER AS ME... NICE...A VERY RICH MAN...

...BUT NOW, IN AUSCHWITZ, MANDELBAUM WAS A **MESS**.

HIS PANTS WERE BIG LIKE FOR 2 PEOPLE, AND HE HAD NOT EVEN A PIECE OF STRING TO MAKE A BELT. HE HAD ALL DAY TO HOLD THEM WITH ONE HAND...

ONE SHOE, HIS FOOT WAS TOO BIG TO GO IN. THIS ALSO HE HAD TO HOLD SO HE COULD FIND MAYBE WITH WHOM TO EXCHANGE IT.

ONE SHOE WAS BIG LIKE A BOAT. BUT **THIS** AT LEAST HE COULD WEAR.

IT WAS WINTER, AND EVERYWHERE HE HAD TO GO AROUND WITH ONE FOOT ONTO THE SNOW.

CAN I USE YOUR SPOON, VLADEK?

OF COURSE, BUT WHERE'S YOURS?

I DROPPED IT, AND BY THE TIME I BENT DOWN, SOMEONE STOLE IT.

FOR A SPOON YOU COULD GET A HALF DAY'S BREAD.

I SPILLED MOST OF MY SOUP, TOO. WHEN I ASKED FOR MORE, THEY **BEAT** ME!

I HOLD ONTO MY BOWL AND MY SHOE FALLS DOWN. I PICK UP THE SHOE AND MY **PANTS** FALL DOWN...

BUT WHAT CAN I DO? I ONLY HAVE TWO HANDS!

MY GOD. PLEASE GOD... HELP ME FIND A PIECE OF STRING AND A SHOE THAT FITS!

BUT HERE GOD DIDN'T COME. WE WERE ALL ON OUR OWN.

SO, MANDELBAUM AND I WERE TWO IN A BED. WE DIDN'T KNOW WHY, SINCE IT WAS SPACES LEFT.

BUT A DAY AFTER, THEY PUSHED IN A SHIPMENT OF MAYBE 400 MORE JEWS THERE.

IT WAS ROOM HARDLY TO MOVE. ONLY TO GO DOWN TO THE TOILET WAS 15 MINUTES WALKING ON THE UNLUCKY ONES SLEEPING ON THE FLOOR.

AND COMING BACK I COULDN'T FIND AGAIN WHERE IS MY BED.

IN THE BARRACK WAS A KAPO – A SUPERVISOR – HE WAS SCREAMING AND KICKING, WHATEVER HE COULD.

LINE UP IN ROWS OF FIVE, YOU SHITS! STAND STRAIGHT!

HE WAS ALSO A PRISONER, A PEASANT FROM THE GERMAN PART OF POLAND.

NOW LIE ON YOUR BELLIES. QUICK!

STAND UP! LIE DOWN!

STAND UP! FASTER!

LIE DOWN!

WE DID SUCH "SPORT" ALL DAY – KICKING, HITTING, YELLING – 'TIL SOME DROPPED DEAD. THEN MORE.

ONE TIME THIS BLOCK SUPERVISOR STARTED SCREAMING ON US:

WHO KNOWS ENGLISH? RAISE YOUR HAND!

(YOU SHOULD RAISE YOUR HAND, VLADEK.)

(NO...)

(I DON'T WANT TO GET TOO CLOSE TO HIS STICK. BESIDES, LOOK AT ALL THE HANDS UP ALREADY...)

MANY FRENCH JEWS HERE KNEW TO SPEAK ENGLISH.

HE TOOK THEM APART—BUT SENT THEM SOON BACK.

WHO KNOWS ENGLISH AND POLISH?

NOW IT WAS VERY FEW HANDS, SO I APPROACHED.

IT WAS 8 OR 9 OF US. EACH HAD TO SPEAK A FEW WORDS.

VHERE... IST... DER PEN?... DER PEN IST... IN... DER TABLE...

NEXT.

WHAT I HEARD THE OTHERS SPEAK I SAW I HAD A CHANCE.

I SPOKE ONLY ENGLISH TO HIM: FOR POLISH, I HAD A **GOOD** ENGLISH

YES. I GAVE PRIVATE LESSONS OF ENGLISH WHEN I LIVED THEN IN CZESTOCHOWA.

HE WANTED TO LEARN HERE **ENGLISH**!

YOU MANAGED TO GET THE BERLITZ BOOKS HERE! YOU STUDIED ALREADY TO CONJUGATE VERBS?

?

AND HE KEPT ME ASIDE THE REST.

LISTEN. THERE ARE TOO MANY PRISONERS HERE. THE S.S. WILL LINE YOU ALL UP TOMORROW.
...BE SURE TO STAND ON THE FAR LEFT.

IN THE MORNING, THE S.S. CHOSE WHO TO TAKE FOR THE DAY TO WORK. WEAK ONES THEY PUT ON THE SIDE TO TAKE AWAY FOREVER. BEFORE THEY CAME TO ME, THEY TOOK ENOUGH.

I KEPT CLOSE TO ME MANDELBAUM. AND WE WENT BACK SAFE INSIDE.

THE KAPO PUSHED THOSE REMAINING TO CLEAN UP IN THE BLOCK.

WAIT! SPIEGELMAN- YOU COME WITH ME!

EVERYONE THEY CALLED BY NUMBER. BUT ME, HE CALLED BY NAME.

SIT HERE... I'LL BE BACK SOON.

HERE I SAW ROLLS! I SAW EGGS! MEAT! COFFEE! ALL THE TABLE FULL! YOU KNOW WHAT IT WAS TO SEE SUCH THINGS?

IT MUST BE IT'S HIS BREAKFAST. SEE HOW HAPPY HE HAS IT HERE!

I WAS AFRAID TO LOOK. I WAS SO HUNGRY, I COULD GRAB ALL OF IT!

WHAT ARE YOU WAITING FOR? SIT DOWN AND EAT!

THIS FOOD, IT WAS FOR ME.

I ATE, ATE, ATE AS HE WATCHED. THEN I TAUGHT HIM A COUPLE HOURS AND WE SPOKE A LITTLE.

BUT WHY ARE YOU STUDYING ENGLISH?

I SPEAK GERMAN AS WELL AS POLISH-THAT'S WHY I'M A KAPO. OTHERWISE I'D BE A NOTHING LIKE YOU...
NOW THE ALLIES ARE BOMBING THE REICH. IF THEY WIN THIS WAR, IT WILL BE WORTH SOMETHING TO KNOW ENGLISH!

WELL, THAT'S ENOUGH FOR TODAY. COME WITH ME.

TAKE OFF ALL YOUR CLOTHES. CHOOSE THINGS THAT FIT.

!

SO I TOOK MYSELF CLOTHES LIKE TAILORED.

I GOT ALSO A PAIR **REAL** SHOES- NOT WOOD BUT LEATHER

ALWAYS I WAS HANDSOME... BUT WITH EVERYTHING FITTED, I LOOKED LIKE A MILLION!

SO. ARE YOU ALL SET?

YES SIR. BUT I HAVE ONE MORE FAVOR TO ASK...

...COULD I ALSO TAKE THIS EXTRA PAIR OF SHOES, A BELT AND A SPOON FOR-

WHAT?!

YOU **JEW!** YOU'VE ONLY BEEN HERE A FEW DAYS AND YOU'RE READY TO DO BUSINESS?!

I HAVE TO ACCOUNT FOR EVERY PAIR OF SHOES IN HERE!

I-I DON'T WANT TO MAKE TROUBLE. YOU'VE BEEN SO **KIND** TO ME... IT WAS FOR MY FRIEND...

I EXPLAINED HIM EVERYTHING ABOUT MANDELBAUM.

WELL... I **COULD** "LOSE" THE BELT AND SPOON - BUT BRING ME YOUR FRIEND'S OLD SHOES TOMORROW - OR **ELSE!**

I'M TELLING YOU - I WAS AMAZING WELL-OFF!

I RAN TO FIND MANDELBAUM...

VLADEK?!!! YOU LOOK LIKE A...A GENERAL!

HAH! NOT QUITE. BUT I'VE BEEN LUCKY, AND I DIDN'T FORGET YOU...

LOOK. I GOT YOU YOUR OWN SPOON.

A SPOON! THANK YOU, VLADEK, THANK YOU.

AND HERE'S A BELT—NOT JUST STRING—A REAL BELT!

OH MY GOD!

AND ONE MORE THING: A PAIR OF WOODEN SHOES THAT WILL FIT YOU!

≟gasp≟

SOB

MY GOD. MY GOD. MY GOD... IT'S A MIRACLE, VLADEK.

GOD SENT SHOES THROUGH YOU.

...HE WAS SO HAPPY, HE WAS CRYING... AND I STARTED ALSO CRYING WITH HIM.

HE WAS SO HAPPY WITH THIS.

...AND THE KAPO KNEW MANDELBAUM WAS MY FRIEND SO HE LEFT HIM ALSO ALONE.

HOW LONG I COULD, I KEPT HIM. BUT A FEW DAYS LATER THE GERMANS CHOSE HIM TO TAKE AWAY TO WORK...

NOBODY COULD HELP THIS. SO. IT WAS FINISHED WITH MANDELBAUM. I NEVER SAW HIM MORE AGAIN.

SO YOU DON'T KNOW WHAT HAPPENED TO MANDELBAUM?

HE GOT KILLED. OR HE DIED. I KNOW THEY *FINISHED* HIM.

MAYBE ON THE WALK TO WORK, A GUARD GRABBED HIS CAP AWAY.

GO GET YOUR CAP-QUICK!

SO WHAT COULD HE DO? HE RAN TO PICK IT UP. AND THE GUARD SHOT ON HIM FOR TRYING TO ESCAPE.

THE GUARD GOT A CONGRATULATIONS AND A FEW DAYS VACATION FOR STOPPING THE ESCAPE.

I DON'T *KNOW* IF THIS WAS HOW IT WAS WITH MANDELBAUM—ONLY THAT VERY OFTEN THEY DID SO...

THEY WANTED ONLY TO FINISH EVERYONE OUT. IT WAS VERY HARD WORK AND VERY LITTLE FOOD.

...MAYBE THEY KICKED AND HIT HIM IN HIS HEAD BECAUSE HE COULDN'T WORK FAST ENOUGH.

...OR MAYBE HE GOT SICK. SO THEY PUT HIM FIRST IN THE "HOSPITAL" AND THEN IN THE OVEN...

YOU SEE HOW THEY DID? AND I HAD IT STILL HAPPY THERE. FOR *ME* IT WAS NOT YET THE END.

NEWCOMERS WERE AFRAID FROM ME. I LOOKED LIKE A *BIG SHOT* AND THE KAPO KEPT ME CLOSE.

THEY'LL WANT 200 WORKERS TOMORROW. I'VE ONLY GOT 180 STILL *REGISTERED* HERE. ...YOU'D BETTER HIDE IN MY ROOM...

FOR OVER TWO MONTHS I STAYED HERE SAFE AND TAUGHT TO HIM ENGLISH.

OF THE GROUP WHEN I ARRIVED, ONLY I REMAINED...

VLADEK, WHAT WAS YOUR PROFESSION BEFORE YOU WERE BROUGHT HERE?

I WORKED IN A *LOT* OF DIFFERENT BUSINESSES. WHY?

I'VE KEPT YOU HERE IN THE "QUARANTINE BLOCK" AS LONG AS I CAN. YOU'LL HAVE TO BE ASSIGNED OUT TO A WORK CREW... SKILLED WORKERS GET BETTER TREATMENT.

I CAN DO *ANYTHING* ONCE I'M SHOWN HOW. IN THE GHETTO I WORKED IN A WOOD SHOP... IN SOSNOWIEC I WAS A TINSMITH.

A TIN-SMITH! I'LL SEE WHAT I CAN DO!

ALWAYS AROUND AUSCHWITZ THEY WERE BUILDING. TO THE ROOFS THEY NEEDED GOOD TINMEN.

I WAS NOT *REALLY* A TINMAN. BUT I KNEW A LITTLE. IN SOSNOWIEC I WAS IN A TIN SHOP REGISTERED TO GET A SAFE WORK PASSPORT, AND I WATCHED HOW THEY WORKED.

THE **Pines**
GUESTS ONLY
No Trespassing

UH-HUH. YOU TOLD ME. WHAT I WANTED TO ASK YOU ABOUT THOUGH, IS WHAT HAPPENED TO MOM WHILE YOU

STOP!...

Pi
GUE
No Tr

WE MUST TURN *QUICK* AND GO BY *THIS* ROAD TO COME TO THE PINES!

HUH?

ERVICE
TRANCE

IN THIS WAY THE HOTEL GUARD CAN'T SEE US, AND WE CAN SIT ON THEIR PATIO. IT'S *PRETTY* THERE TO SIT. I COME ALMOST EVERY DAY IN THIS WAY.

SOMETIMES I GET HERE FREE DANCING LESSONS, OR THEY HAVE FOR THE GUESTS FREE BINGO GAMES AND PRIZES.

36

DOWNSTAIRS IS A GYM WITH A STEAM ROOM AND A WHIRL-POOL... MAYBE I CAN TAKE YOU IN THERE TOMORROW.

NO THANKS. AREN'T YOU AFRAID YOU'LL GET CAUGHT TRESPASSING?

FEH. FROM OUR BUNGALOWS EVERYBODY COMES HERE ALWAYS, OR TO BRICKMAN'S HOTEL UP THE ROAD.

...I LIKE BETTER THE PINES. ONLY IT'S THAT IN THE GYM HERE YOU CAN'T HAVE A LOCKER WITHOUT GIVING A ROOM KEY.

LOOK. THEY'RE GIVING NOW CARDS FOR BINGO. YOU WANT WE'LL PLAY?

UH-UH. I'LL PUT IN A NEW TAPE AND WE CAN CONTINUE.

I WON HERE A BINGO GAME ONE TIME. THE WINNER GOT A PRIZE OVER TO HIS ROOM. ...ONLY IT WAS, I HAD NO ROOM.

BEHIND ME SAT A YOUNG LADY WHAT GOT SO DISAPPOINTED THAT SHE LOST— SHE HAD JUST ONE NUMBER AWAY...

...SO I GAVE TO HER MY CARD AND SAID: "I DON'T CARE FOR SUCH PRIZES—YOU GO UP TO BE THE WINNER."...WAS SHE HAPPY.

DID YOU TELL HER YOU WEREN'T A GUEST HERE?

WHY TO TELL?? THIS WASN'T HER BUSINESS.

YOU KNOW, IN TOWN IS A BINGO PLACE- 50¢ A CARD. MALA LIKED SOMETIMES TO GO... AND I SAID TO HER, "FOR WHAT? FOR THE COFFEE THEY GIVE AFTER? BINGO WE CAN PLAY AT THE PINES, AND BETTER COFFEE WE HAVE AT HOME!"

...B-5. G-22...

BINGO!

CHAPTER TWO

Time flies...

Vladek died of congestive heart failure on August 18, 1982...

Françoise and I stayed with him in the Catskills back in August 1979.

Vladek started working as a tinman in Auschwitz in the spring of 1944...

I started working on this page at the very end of February 1987.

In May 1987 Françoise and I are expecting a baby...

Between May 16, 1944, and May 24, 1944 over 100,000 Hungarian Jews were gassed in Auschwitz...

In September 1986, after 8 years of work, the first part of MAUS was published. It was a critical and commercial success.

At least fifteen foreign editions are coming out. I've gotten 4 serious offers to turn my book into a T.V. special or movie. (I don't wanna.)

In May 1968 my mother killed herself. (She left no note.)

Lately I've been feeling depressed.

Alright Mr. Spiegelman... We're ready to shoot!...

41

Tell our viewers what message you want them to get from your book?

a message? I dunno...

I-I never thought of reducing it to a message. I mean, I wasn't trying to CONVINCE anybody of anything. I just wanted—

Your book is being translated into German...

Many younger Germans have had it up to HERE with Holocaust stories. These things happened before they were even born. Why should THEY feel guilty?

Who am I to say?...

But a lot of the corporations that flourished in Nazi Germany are richer than ever. I dunno... Maybe EVERYONE has to feel guilty. EVERYONE! FOREVER!

Okay... Let's talk about Israel...

If your book was about ISRAELI Jews, what kind of animal would you draw?

I have no idea. ...porcupines?

Excuse me...

Artie, baby. Check out this licensing deal. You get 50% of the profits. We'll make a million. Your dad would be proud!

HUH?

MAUS
YOU'VE READ THE BOOK
NOW BUY THE VEST!

So, whaddya WANT— a bigger percentage? Hey, we can talk.

I want... ABSOLUTION. No... No... I want...I want.. my MOMMY!

Could you tell our audience if drawing MAUS was cathartic? Do you feel better now?

WAH!

≷whew.≷ they're gone. Sometimes I just don't feel like a functioning adult.

I can't believe I'm gonna be a father in a couple of months.* My father's ghost still hangs over me.

* NADJA MOULY SPIEGELMAN. BORN 5/13/87

It's 9:30 p.m. already. I've gotta head uptown for my appointment with Pavel.

Pavel is my shrink. He sees patients at night.

He's a Czech Jew, a survivor of Terezin and Auschwitz. I see him once a week.

His place is overrun with stray dogs and cats.

Hi Art. Come on in.

Can I mention this, or does it completely louse up my metaphor?

So, how are you feeling?

Completely messed up. I mean, things couldn't be going better with my "career," or at home, but mostly I feel like crying.

I can't work. My time is being sucked up by interviews and business propositions I can't deal with.

But even when I'm left alone I'm totally BLOCKED. Instead of working on my book I just lie on my couch for hours and stare at a small grease spot on the upholstery.

FRAMED PHOTO OF PET CAT. REALLY!

43

Panel 1: Somehow my arguments with my father have lost a little of their urgency... and Auschwitz just seems too scary to think about... so I just *LIE* there...

Panel 2: It sounds like you're feeling remorse—maybe you believe you exposed your father to ridicule.

Maybe. But I tried to be fair and still show how angry I felt.

Panel 3: Even so, EVERY boy when he's little, looks up to his father.

That sounds true, but it's hard for me to remember...

Panel 4: Mainly I remember ARGUING with him... and being told that I couldn't do anything as well as he could.

And now that you're becoming successful, you feel bad about proving your father wrong.

Panel 5: No matter what I accomplish, it doesn't seem like much compared to surviving Auschwitz.

But you weren't in Auschwitz... you were in Rego Park.

Panel 6: Maybe your father needed to show that he was always right—that he could always SURVIVE—because he felt GUILTY about surviving.

maybe.

Panel 7: And he took his guilt out on YOU, where it was safe... on the REAL survivor.

um... Tell me, do you feel any guilt about surviving the camps?

Panel 8: No... just sadness.

So, do you ADMIRE your father for surviving?

Well.... Sure. I know there was a lot of LUCK involved, but he WAS amazingly present-minded and resourceful...

Then you think it's admirable to survive. Does that mean it's NOT admirable to NOT survive?

whoosh.

I-I think I see what you mean. It's as if life equals winning, so death equals losing.

Yes. Life always takes the side of life, and somehow the victims are blamed. But it wasn't the BEST people who survived, nor did the best ones die. It was RANDOM!

Sigh. I'm not talking about YOUR book now, but look at how many books have already been written about the Holocaust. What's the point? People haven't changed....

Maybe they need a newer, bigger Holocaust.

Anyway, the victims who died can never tell THEIR side of the story, so maybe it's better not to have any more stories.

Uh-huh. Samuel Beckett once said: "Every word is like an unnecessary stain on silence and nothingness."

Yes.

On the other hand, he SAID it.

He was right. Maybe you can include it in your book.

My book? Hah! What book?? Some part of me doesn't want to draw or think about Auschwitz. I can't visualize it clearly, and I can't BEGIN to imagine what it felt like.

What Auschwitz felt like? Hmm... How can I explain?...

BOO!

YIII!

It felt a little like *that*. But ALWAYS! From the moment you got to the gate until the very end.

So, what part of your idea are you trying to visualize?

My father worked in a tin shop near the camp. I have no idea what kind of tools and stuff to draw. There's no documentation.

Let's see. There would be a cutter—like a giant paper cutter—and maybe an electric drill press or two.

How do you KNOW that?

Oh, I worked in a tool and die shop in Czechoslovakia when I was a kid.

But it's getting late now, and I still have to walk my dogs.

Okay, I'll see you in a week...

Gee. I don't understand exactly why...

but these sessions with Pavel somehow make me feel better...

Maybe I could show the tin shop and not draw the drill press. I hate to draw machinery.

46

And so...

CLIK ...THEN, WHEN I CAME OUT FROM THE HOSPITAL, RIGHT AWAY SHE STARTED **AGAIN** THAT I CHANGE MY WILL!

PLEASE POP. THE TAPE'S ON. LET'S CONTINUE...

I WAS STILL SO SICK AND TIRED. AND TO HAVE PEACE ONLY, I AGREED, TO MAKE IT LEGAL SHE BROUGHT RIGHT TO MY BED A **NOTARY**.

LET'S GET BACK TO AUSCHWITZ...

FIFTEEN DOLLARS HE CHARGED TO COME! IF SHE WAITED ONLY A WEEK UNTIL I WAS STRONGER, I'D GO TO THE BANK AND TAKE A NOTARY FOR ONLY A QUARTER!

ENOUGH! TELL ME ABOUT AUSCHWITZ!

sigh

YOU WERE TELLING ME HOW YOUR KAPO TRIED TO GET YOU WORK AS A TINSMITH...

YAH. EVERY DAY I WORKED THERE RIGHT OUTSIDE FROM THE CAMP...

THE CHIEF OF THE TINMEN IT WAS A RUSSIAN JEW NAMED YIDL.

BAH! YOU'RE NO TINSMITH. YOU CAN'T EVEN **CUT** IT RIGHT.

BUT THIS IS HOW I'VE **ALWAYS** DONE IT!...

I'VE ONLY BEEN A TINSMITH FOR A FEW YEARS. IF YOU SHOW ME HOW **YOU** WANT IT CUT I CAN LEARN QUICKLY.

HAH! YOU NEVER DID AN HONEST DAY'S WORK IN YOUR WHOLE LIFE, SPIEGELMAN! I KNOW ALL ABOUT YOU...

I DON'T KNOW WHERE FROM HE HEARD STORIES ABOUT ME.

YOU OWNED BIG FACTORIES AND EXPLOITED YOUR WORKERS, YOU DIRTY CAPITALIST!

HE WAS A **COMMUNIST**, THIS YIDL.

PFUI! THEY SEND DREK LIKE YOU HERE WHILE THEY SEND REAL TINMEN UP THE CHIMNEY. WATCH OUT. I'VE GOT MY EYE ON YOU!

I WAS AFRAID. HE COULD REALLY **DO** ME SOMETHING.

WITH THE OTHER BOYS THERE, I GOT ALONG FINE.

DON'T WORRY... YOU JUST HAVE TO KNOW HOW TO HANDLE YIDL...

BRING HIM A FEW EGGS, SOME BUTTER OR CHEESE...

YOU'LL SEE. HE'LL SING A DIFFERENT TUNE.

HA! AND WHERE DO I GET ALL THIS FOOD?

JUST KEEP YOUR EYES OPEN. YOU CAN ORGANIZE THINGS WITH THE POLES HERE.

POLES FROM NEARBY THEY HIRED TO WORK ALSO HERE — NOT PRISONERS, BUT SPECIALIST BUILDING WORKERS...

(PSST — I CAN GET YOU A FINE GOLD WATCH FOR A POUND OF SAUSAGE AND SIX EGGS.)

(AGREED.)

THEY HAD **NOTHING**, ONLY FOOD FROM THEIR FARMS. THEY WERE HAPPY TO MAKE EXCHANGES.

THE HEAD GUY FROM THE AUSCHWITZ LAUNDRY WAS A FINE FELLOW WHAT KNEW WELL MY FAMILY BEFORE THE WAR...

FROM HIM I GOT CIVILIAN **CLOTHINGS** TO SMUGGLE OUT BELOW MY UNIFORM. I WAS SO THIN THE GUARDS DIDN'T SEE IF I WORE EXTRA.

HERE YIDL. I'VE GOT A BIG PIECE OF CHEESE FOR YOU.

A GIFT? VERY NICE, SPIEGELMAN.

AND WHAT ELSE DO YOU HAVE THERE? A LOAF OF BREAD? YOU'RE A RICH MAN!

WAIT! I NEED THAT TO PAY OFF THE GUY WHO HELPED ME ORGANIZE THE CHEESE!

HMPH.

HE WAS SO GREEDY, YIDL, HE WANTED I RISK ONLY FOR HIM EVERYTHING. I TOO HAD TO EAT.

EVERYBODY WAS SO HUNGRY ALWAYS, WE DIDN'T KNOW EVEN WHAT WE ARE DOING...

IN THE MORNING FOR BREAK-FAST WE GOT ONLY A BITTER DRINK MADE FROM ROOTS.

I WOKE BEFORE EVERYBODY TO HAVE TIME TO THE TOILET AND FIND STILL SOME TEA LEFT.

ONE TIME A DAY THEY GAVE A SOUP FROM TURNIPS. TO STAND NEAR THE FIRST OF THE LINE WAS NO GOOD. YOU GOT ONLY WATER.

MIX IT! MIX IT!

NEAR THE END WAS BETTER - SOLID THINGS TO THE BOTTOM FLOATED.

BUT TOO FAR TO THE END IT WAS ALSO NO GOOD

...BECAUSE MANY TIMES IT COULD BE NO SOUP ANYMORE.

AND ONE TIME EACH DAY THEY GAVE TO US A SMALL BREAD, CRUNCHY LIKE GLASS.

THE FLOUR THEY MIXED WITH SAWDUST TOGETHER - WE GOT ONE LITTLE BRICK OF THIS WHAT HAD TO LAST THE FULL DAY.

MOST GOBBLED IT RIGHT AWAY, BUT ALWAYS I SAVED A HALF FOR LATER.

AND IN THE EVENING WE GOT A SPOILED CHEESE OR JAM. IF WE WERE LUCKY A COUPLE TIMES A WEEK WE GOT A SAUSAGE BIG LIKE TWO OF MY FINGERS. ONLY THIS MUCH WE GOT

IF YOU ATE HOW THEY GAVE YOU, IT WAS JUST ENOUGH TO DIE MORE SLOWLY.

EACH MORNING AND EVENING THEY MADE AN APPEL. THEY COUNTED THE LIVE ONES AND DEAD ONES TO SEE IT WASN'T ANY MISSING...

WE STOOD SOMETIMES THE WHOLE NIGHT WHILE THEY COUNTED AGAIN AND AGAIN.

ON OUR APPELS IT WAS ONE OLD GUY THERE, ALWAYS HE WAS COMPLAINING...

I DON'T BELONG HERE WITH ALL THESE YIDS AND POLACKS! I'M A **GERMAN** LIKE YOU!

I HAVE MEDALS FROM THE KAISER. MY SON IS A GERMAN SOLDIER!

ONLY THEY HIT HIM AND THEY LAUGHED.

WAS HE REALLY A GERMAN?

WHO KNOWS... IT WAS GERMAN PRISONERS ALSO... BUT FOR THE GERMANS THIS GUY WAS JEWISH!

ON ONE APPEL HE DIDN'T STAND SO STRAIGHT AND A GUARD DRAGGED HIM AWAY. I HEARD HE PUSHED HIM DOWN AND JUMPED HARD ON HIS NECK...

OR THEY SENT HIM TO THE GAS, I DON'T REMEMBER, BUT THEY FINISHED HIM AND HE NEVER ANYMORE COMPLAINED.

51

COME... IT'S TIME NOW WE'LL HURRY FOR LUNCH HOME TO THE BUNGALOW.

SO YOU WERE ACTUALLY IN *TOUCH* WITH ANJA IN BIRKENAU?

YAH. FROM MANCIE I HAD A REAL CONTACT WITH MOTHER, UNTIL LATER I COULD BRING ANJA TO—

WAIT! WHO'S MANCIE?

SHE WAS A HUNGARIAN, MANCIE, WHO WORKED SOMETIMES THERE. BEAUTIFUL. A TALL BLONDE GIRL. AND CLEVER.

REST BEHIND THAT STACK OF WOOD. I'LL WARN YOU IF A GUARD COMES CLOSE.

SHE HAD A LOVER, I HEARD LATER, AN S.S. MAN. HE GOT FOR HER A GOOD POSITION OVER 10 OR 12 OTHER GIRLS FROM BIRKENAU.

(PSST, MISS—UP HERE! I SEE HOW KIND YOU ARE. HELP ME. PLEASE!)

HUH? (WHAT DO YOU WANT?)

(NOTHING FOR ME, BUT I'M AFRAID FOR MY WIFE IN BIRKENAU. CAN YOU FIND OUT IF SHE'S STILL ALIVE?)

I TOLD TO HER ANJA'S NAME AND NUMBER.

(I'VE SAVED SOME FOOD. I CAN PAY FOR YOUR HELP.)

(KEEP YOUR FOOD. WE'LL BE WORKING HERE AGAIN IN A FEW DAYS. I'LL SEE WHAT I CAN FIND OUT.)

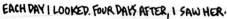

EACH DAY I LOOKED. FOUR DAYS AFTER, I SAW HER.

I MET A WOMAN NAMED ANJA FROM SOSNOWIEC. SHE'S VERY FRAIL...

SHE SPOKE OVER TO ONE OF HER WORKERS; I SPOKE ONLY TO MY TIN SO NOBODY WILL NOTICE.

SOMEONE TOLD HER THAT HER HUSBAND IS STILL ALIVE AND SHE STARTED SOBBING WITH JOY.

I HEARD THIS, AND I STARTED ALSO CRYING A LITTLE. AND MANCIE, SHE TOO STARTED CRYING.

A FEW DAYS AFTER, MANCIE AGAIN CAME THERE.

I PUT SOME "GARBAGE" UNDER A ROCK NEAR THE DOORWAY.

SHE BROUGHT TO ME A LETTER— A REAL LETTER!—FROM ANJA.

"I MISS YOU," SHE WROTE TO ME. "EACH DAY I THINK TO RUN INTO THE ELECTRIC WIRES AND FINISH EVERYTHING. BUT TO KNOW YOU ARE ALIVE IT GIVES ME STILL TO HOPE..."

SHE TOLD ME HER KAPO WAS VERY MEAN ON HER AND GAVE WORK ANJA REALLY COULDN'T DO.

EVEN FOR ME SUCH CANS WERE HEAVY, AND FOR ANJA—SHE WAS SO SMALL—IT WAS IMPOSSIBLE.

LIKE TO RUN FROM THE KITCHEN WITH THE BIG CANS OF SOUP.

SHE COULDN'T HOLD WELL HER END. ALWAYS SHE SPILLED.

THE KAPO BEAT ANJA VERY HARD BUT KEPT HER TO THIS JOB.

AND IF ANJA SPILLED OVER ALL FROM THE SOUP, THEN NOBODY GOT WHAT TO EAT, ESPECIALLY ANJA.

I WROTE TO HER: "I THINK OF YOU ALWAYS," AND SENT WITH MANCIE TWO PIECES OF BREAD.

IF THE S.S. WOULD SEE SHE IS TAKING FOOD INTO THE CAMP, RIGHT AWAY THEY WILL KILL HER.

BUT ALWAYS SHE TOOK.

SO SHE SAID: "IF A COUPLE IS LOVING EACH OTHER SO MUCH, I MUST HELP HOWEVER I CAN."

EACH DAY I MARCHED TO WORK AND HOPED AGAIN I'LL SEE MANCIE...

SHE COULD HAVE MORE NEWS OF ANJA.

I JUST READ ABOUT THE CAMP ORCHESTRA THAT PLAYED AS YOU MARCHED OUT THE GATE...

AN ORCHESTRA?..

NO. I REMEMBER ONLY *MARCHING*, NOT ANY ORCHESTRAS...

FROM THE GATE GUARDS TOOK US OVER TO THE WORK-SHOP. HOW COULD IT BE THERE AN ORCHESTRA?

I DUNNO, BUT IT'S VERY WELL DOCUMENTED...

NO. AT THE GATE I HEARD ONLY GUARDS SHOUTING.

DID YOU EVER *TALK* WITH ANY OF THE GUARDS?

ACH! WE WERE BELOW THEIR DIGNITY. WE WERE NOT EVEN MEN. BUT IT WAS ONE GUY...

IF HE SPOKE OF COURSE I ANSWERED. HE HAD EVEN A LITTLE HEART.

AAH. GUTEN MORGEN. THIS SPRING AIR REMINDS ME OF HOME... OF NUREMBURG...

YES. I WAS THERE ONCE. IT'S A BEAUTIFUL CITY.

AND IF HE LIKED ME, MAYBE SOMEDAY HE WON'T SHOOT ME

ONE TIME HE WAS MISSING A FEW DAYS...

YOU LOOK PALE. WERE YOU SICK HERR SOLDAT?

NO... I WAS.... WORKING ... IN BIRKENAU.

YES... I'VE HEARD ABOUT WHAT GOES ON THERE...

SHUT UP!

AND HE WAS *AFRAID* ANYMORE TO SPEAK.

WHEN I VISITED TO ANJA THERE, I SAW WITH MY OWN EYES HOW IT WAS...

YOU *SAW* ANJA?

YA. EVERY FEW DAYS IT CAME AN S.S. COMMISSION TO THE TIN SHOP...

YOU HAVE MORE WORKERS THAN YOU NEED HERE...

GIVE US 10 PRISONERS TO TAKE BACK TO THE MAIN CAMP FOR OTHER WORK.

WELL ...TAKE *THAT* ONE ... AND THAT ONE--

AND -- WAIT! DON'T TAKE *HIM*! HE'S ONE OF MY BEST ROOFERS... TAKE THAT ONE...AND THAT ONE--

THE UNLUCKY ONES WENT OVER FOR *BAD* JOBS, BUT ME YIDL KEPT PROTECTED.

...SEND A CREW TO SECTOR BIb IN BIRKENAU. SOME OF THE ROOFS IN THE WOMEN'S CAMP HAVE COLLAPSED.

LET ME GO TO BIRKENAU. I'VE NEVER SEEN IT.

GO, SPIEGELMAN, AND DON'T COME BACK FOR ALL I CARE. BAH! I GIVE UP MY BEST TINMEN, AND YOU I SAVE. **WHY?!**

SO I MARCHED WITH A FEW TIN-MEN OVER TO BIRKENAU. I CAME THE FIRST TIME IN SUMMER 1944.

THOUSANDS--HUNDREDS OF THOUSANDS OF HUN-GARIANS WERE ARRIV-ING THERE AT THIS TIME.

INSIDE THE CAMP WE CALLED OUT. MAYBE SOMEBODY KNEW IF OUR LOVED ONES ARE HERE ALIVE.

EVA. EVA GOLDBERG FROM LODZ!

ANJA ZYLBERBERG! FROM SOSNOWIEC!

MY GOD. THAT'S VLADEK! I'LL GO FIND ANJA!

I WAS SO HAPPY. SOMEONE BROUGHT SOMEHOW ANJA OVER

DON'T LOOK UP, DARLING. A GUARD MAY SPOT US.

SHE LOOKED SO LIKE A SKELETON.

DID MANCIE BRING YOU MY LETTERS?

YES. AND WHEN SHE CAN, SHE GETS ME JOBS IN THE KITCHEN!

MY FRIENDS WAIT OUTSIDE AND I BRING THEM SCRAPS.

NO! SAVE YOUR SCRAPS! WHAT IF YOU LOSE THAT JOB? WHAT IF SOMETHING HAPPENS TO MANCIE?

DON'T WORRY ABOUT FRIENDS. BELIEVE ME, THEY DON'T WORRY ABOUT YOU. THEY JUST WORRY ABOUT GETTING A BIGGER SHARE OF YOUR FOOD!

BUT MY FRIENDS ARE ALWAYS HUNGRY, AND I—I DON'T HAVE MUCH OF AN APPETITE.

I BEG YOU, ANJA—KEEP YOURSELF STRONG. FOR MY SAKE.

JUST SEEING YOU AGAIN GIVES ME STRENGTH.

I HAVE TO GO BEFORE ANYONE NOTICES I'M MISSING.

I.... I THINK ABOUT YOU ...ALWAYS.

I WAS A *FEW* TIMES IN BIRKENAU, AND ONCE I HAD *REALLY* TROUBLES. I WAS GOING FROM WORK AND PASSED BY ANJA...

VLADEK! VLADEK! VLADEK!

ANJA! DARLING! DID YOU GET THE FOOD I SENT YOU?

YES. YOU ALWAYS ARRANGE MIRACLES.

I THINK ABOUT YOU ...ALWAYS.

WE SPOKE A MINUTE ONLY AND I WENT ON MY WAY.

A GUARD SCREAMED TO ME:

HALT!

WHO WERE YOU TALKING TO?

N-NOBODY...

A STRANGER ASKED IF I KNEW HER BROTHERS IN AUSCHWITZ. I DIDN'T KNOW ANYTHING, SO I HARDLY ANSWERED.

GET INSIDE!

WHEN I'M FINISHED WITH YOU, YOU'LL KNOW *SOMETHING*, JEWISH PIMP! YOU'RE NOT HERE TO FLIRT AND GOSSIP.

COUNT THE BLOWS. IF YOU LOSE COUNT—I'LL START AGAIN!

EINS! ZWEI! DREI!

SO HE BEAT ME, WHAT CAN I TELL YOU? ONLY, THANK GOD, ANJA DIDN'T GET *ALSO* SUCH A BEATING. SHE WOULDN'T LIVE.

THE NEXT DAYS IT WAS HARD TO GO WORK, BUT TO GO TO THE HOSPITAL, I COULD EASY NOT COME AGAIN OUT.

IT WASN'T A PLACE WITH MEDICINES, ONLY A PLACE FULL WITH PRISONERS TOO SICK TO GO WORK.

EACH DAY IT WAS SELEKTIONS. THE DOCTORS CHOSE OUT THE WEAKER ONES TO GO AND DIE.

IN THE WHOLE CAMP WAS SELEKTIONS. I WENT TWO TIMES IN FRONT OF DR. MENGELE.

WE STOOD WITHOUT ANYTHING, STRAIGHT LIKE A SOLDIER. HE GLANCED AND SAID: "FACE LEFT!"

THEY LOOKED TO SEE IF IT WAS SORES OR PIMPLES ON THE BODY. THEN AGAIN: "FACE LEFT!"

THEY LOOKED TO SEE IF EATING NO FOOD MADE YOU TOO SKINNY...

FACE LEFT!

IF YOU HAD STILL A HEALTHY BODY TO WORK, THEY PASSED YOU THROUGH AND GAVE YOU ANOTHER UNIFORM UNTIL IT CAME THE NEXT SELEKTION...

WHEN FIRST I CAME I WAS VERY STRONG THEN, AND CAME WELL TO THE GOOD SIDE.

THE ONES THAT HAD NOT SO LUCKY THE S.S. WROTE DOWN THEIR NUMBER AND SENT TO THE OTHER SIDE.

THE SECOND SELEKTION I WAS IN THE BARRACK. IN THE BED UP FROM ME WAS A FINE BOY, A BELGIAN.

I DREAMED MY WIFE WAS ALIVE. SHE WAS COOKING A GIANT ROAST WITH THICK GRAVY AND FRIED—

STOP, FELIX! DON'T THINK ABOUT FOOD!

WE WERE EXPECTING DINNER GUESTS. WE WAITED AND WAITED...THEN THE GONG RANG. I WOKE UP WITHOUT EVEN TASTING THE—

BLOCKSPERRE!

A "BLOCKSPERRE," THIS MEANT YOU MUST NOT STEP OUT FROM THE ROOM.

THEY TOOK THEN THE JEWS TO A SELEKTION. I CAME AGAIN TO THE GOOD SIDE, BUT THIS BELGIAN, HE HAD MAYBE A RASH, AND THEY WROTE HIS NUMBER...

ANY TIME THEY COULD TAKE HIM. ALL NIGHT HE CRIED AND SCREAMED.

AAWOOWWAH!

HERE FELIX. HAVE A PIECE OF BREAD...

SOB

LOOK. THEY'RE GOING TO KILL ALL OF US HERE EVENTUALLY.. YOU THIS WEEK, ME THE NEXT...

...NONE OF US CAN ESCAPE IT. YOU MUST BE BRAVE... AND, WHO KNOWS, MAYBE IT'S NOT EVEN YOUR TURN YET...

SO HE CALMED A LITTLE...

BUT LATER HE AGAIN STARTED..

AWOOOWAA!

WHAT COULD I DO? I COULDN'T TELL TO THE GERMANS THEY WON'T TAKE HIM... AND THE NEXT DAY, THEY TOOK.

SO... IN THE TINSHOP I HAD STILL THE SAME STORY WITH YIDL.

ONLY ONE APPLE FOR ME TODAY? IS BUSINESS BAD, MR. CAPITALIST?

WHAT HAPPENED TO THE SHOEMAKER WHO WORKED IN THERE?

A LOT OF THE POLISH PRISONERS WERE SENT TO CAMPS INSIDE THE REICH. THEY TOOK SOME OF MY BOYS TOO.

I RAN TO THE KAPO IN CHARGE FROM ALL THE SHOP.

DO YOU NEED A NEW SHOEMAKER?

SURE. THE S.S. TOOK THE OLD ONE AWAY, BUT THEY'RE STILL BRINGING SHOES IN!

YOU KNOW, I'VE BEEN A SHOEMAKER SINCE CHILDHOOD.

YOU DON'T *LOOK* LIKE A SHOEMAKER TO ME... YOU'RE A *TINMAN*!

DO I HAVE TO HAVE IT WRITTEN ON MY FOREHEAD?

ALRIGHT, THEN... FIX *THIS*!

I LEARNED A LITTLE SHOE FIXING WATCHING HOW THEY WORKED WHEN I WAS WITH MY COUSIN MILOCH, THERE IN THE GHETTO SHOE SHOP.

TO FIX SUCH AN OPENED SOLE I KNEW TO TAKE A DOUBLE THREAD SMEARED WITH WAX.

...MAKE THEN A HOLE AND PUSH THE THREAD HALF WAY ONLY.

AND ON THE UPPER PART PUT TWO HOLES EVEN TO THE SOLE...

BRING THE THREAD THEN THROUGH *THESE* HOLES.

CROSS THE THREAD FROM THE TOP AND BOTTOM, *BOTH* ENDS THROUGH A NEW HOLE IN THE SOLE AND REPEAT SO UNTIL THE SHOE IS CLOSED.

...AND SO IT'S MADE, YOU CAN'T EVEN *SEE* IT HAS STITCHES!

YOU'RE BETTER THAN OUR *LAST* SHOEMAKER!

YOU SEE? IT'S GOOD TO KNOW HOW TO DO *EVERYTHING*!

SO, NOW I WAS A SHOEMAKER. I HAD HERE A WARM AND PRIVATE ROOM WHERE TO SIT...

OFFICIALS LIKED BETTER IF I FIX THEIR SHOES THAN TO SEND TO THE BIG SHOP INSIDE CAMP.

HA! I KNEW YOU WERE AN EXPERT TINMAN, BUT I NEVER KNEW YOU HAD SO MANY OTHER TALENTS!

AND HERE I DIDN'T HAVE ANYMORE TO WORRY WILL YIDL GIVE ME OUT.

THIS IS A NEW BOOT. I DON'T WANT YOUR REPAIR TO SHOW.

IT'S A BAD RIP... I'LL DO MY BEST.

IF IT DOESN'T LOOK BRAND NEW BY TOMORROW YOU WON'T BE HERE ANYMORE. UNDERSTAND ME?

I KNEW TO FIX SOLES AND HEELS, BUT WHAT THIS GESTAPO WANTED, IT NEEDED A SPECIALIST.

SO, GOING FROM WORK, I HID THIS BOOT TO SNEAK IT TO A REAL SHOEMAKER IN AUSCHWITZ.

CAN YOU FIX THIS? I'LL GIVE YOU A DAY'S RATION OF BREAD.

FOR A DAY'S RATION OF BREAD I CAN FIX ANYTHING!

I WATCHED CAREFUL HOW HE DID, SO NEXT TIME I CAN SAVE MYSELF SUCH A BREAD.

NEXT DAY I HAD THE BOOT READY FOR THIS GESTAPO.

HE LEFT THE BOOT AND WENT WITHOUT ONE WORD.

AND HE CAME BACK WITH A WHOLE SAUSAGE.

HMM

YOU DID A GOOD JOB.

YOU KNOW WHAT THIS WAS, A WHOLE SAUSAGE? YOU CAN'T IMAGINE! I CUT WITH A SHOE KNIFE AND ATE SO FAST I WAS A LITTLE SICK AFTER.

I COULDN'T ANYMORE MAKE A BUSINESS SMUG- GLING WITH POLISH WORKERS FROM HERE AS A SHOEMAKER, BUT STILL I WAS WELL-OFF...

THE GESTAPO WHAT I FIXED HIS BOOT RECOM- MENDED ME, SO HIS FRIENDS WANTED I'LL FIX ALSO THEIR SHOES AND PAID ME FOOD.

I SHARED SOMETIMES TO THE KAPO IN CHARGE.

I JUST ORGANIZED SOME EGGS-WANT ONE?

WHAT A FRIENDLY JEW! SURE-WE CAN COOK THEM ON MY HEATER.

IF YOU WANT TO LIVE, IT'S GOOD TO BE FRIENDLY.

AND HERE'S A LITTLE BREAD FOR OUR MEAL.

GREAT! SAY, WHAT ARE ALL THOSE NEW BUILDINGS THEY'RE PUTTING UP THERE?

JUST SOME NEW WORKSHOPS. THEY'RE EXPANDING THE *UNION WERKE* MUNI- TIONS FACTORY...

AND THEY'RE PUTTING UP SOME BARRACKS TO MOVE SOME WOMEN WORKERS FROM BIRKENAU OVER HERE.

M-MY WIFE IS IN BIR- KENAU. MAYBE I COULD GET HER INTO ONE OF THOSE BARRACKS!

HAH! IMPOSSIBLE! IT WOULD COST A **FORTUNE** IN BRIBES!

HE UNWRAPPED SOME CHEESE AND ATE HIMSELF A PIECE.

PLEASE, COULD I HAVE THAT PIECE OF PAPER?

WELL, SURE. I CAN LET YOU HAVE THE PAPER— BUT NOT THE CHEESE!

I NEEDED TO WRITE OVER TO ANJA!

I THOUGHT ONLY HOW HAPPY IT WOULD BE TO HAVE ANJA SO NEAR TO ME IN THESE NEW BARRACKS.

IT COULD BE "ARRANGED" FOR 100 CIGARETTES AND A BOTTLE VODKA, BUT THIS WAS A FORTUNE.

one day's bread. = 3 cigarettes

200 cigarettes = 1 bottle of vodka

HOW COULD YOU GET CIGARETTES?

EACH WEEK TO THE WORKERS, THEY GAVE US THREE.

THEY ISSUED A LUXURY LIKE THAT?

YA. AND IF YOU DON'T SMOKE YOU CAN EXCHANGE FOR BREAD.

I STARVED A LITTLE TO PAY TO BRING ANJA OVER.

ALL WHAT I ORGANIZED I KEPT IN A BOX UNDER MY MATTRESS.

BUT, WHEN I CAME BACK ONE TIME FROM WORK...

IT—IT'S GONE!

I'M TELLING YOU I WANTED TO CRY.

YOU LEFT THE BOX IN THE BARRACK? HOW COULD IT NOT BE TAKEN?

I DIDN'T THINK ON IT...

BUT EVERYONE WAS STARVING TO DEATH! SIGH-I GUESS I JUST DON'T UNDERSTAND.

YES... ABOUT AUSCHWITZ, NOBODY CAN UNDERSTAND.

SO... I SAVED A SECOND TIME A FORTUNE, AND GAVE OVER BRIBES TO BRING ANJA CLOSE TO ME. AND IN THE START OF OCTOBER, 1944, I SAW A FEW THOUSAND WOMEN IN THESE NEW BARRACKS...

AND WITH THEM WAS ANJA. THIS I ARRANGED. IT WAS THE ONLY TIME I WAS HAPPY IN AUSCHWITZ.

WHEN NOBODY SAW I WENT BACK AND FORTH UNTIL I SAW HER FROM FAR GOING TO MAKE MUNITIONS...

SHE WENT ALSO BACK AND FORTH UNTIL IT WAS SAFE TO APPROACH OVER TO MY FOOD PACKAGES...

BUT ONE TIME, IT WAS VERY BAD.

HEY, YOU! STOP!

DROP THAT PACKAGE AND STOP RIGHT THERE!

STOP!

SHE RAN—SHE DIDN'T KNOW WHERE—INTO HER OWN BLOCK.

ONLY A FRIEND FROM ANJA WAS THERE AS A ROOM CLEANER...

H-HIDE ME, LONIA, *QUICK!*

GET UNDER ONE OF THE BLANKETS!

I KNOW YOU'RE IN HERE SOMEPLACE, AND WHEN I FIND YOU, I'LL *KILL YOU* RIGHT HERE ON THE SPOT!

IT WAS SEVERAL ROOMS THERE, AND HUNDREDS OF BEDS. IN ONE, ANJA LAY SHAKING, AFRAID TO *BREATHE* EVEN.

I'LL KILL YOU! KILL YOU!

FOR MAYBE AN HOUR, LIKE CRAZY SHE RAN FROM ROOM TO ROOM, THROWING UPSIDE DOWN THE BEDS.

BAH! GET ALL THE BEDS IN ORDER BEFORE THE APPEL.

OKAY, ANJA. IT'S SAFE TO COME OUT NOW.

BUT THIS WASN'T YET OVER.

ON THE EVENING APPEL SHE CAME AGAIN THIS KAPO.

THE PRISONER I CHASED THIS AFTER-NOON WILL NOW STEP FORWARD!

BUT MOTHER DIDN'T STEP OUT.

IT WILL BE BETTER FOR YOU IF YOU STEP OUT THAN IF I FIND YOU!

SHE CAME BACK AND FORTH, LOOKING IN EACH FACE, BUT WITH THE STRIPES EVERYONE LOOKED ALL THE SAME.

IF YOU KNOW WHO SHE IS, PUSH HER FORWARD OR YOU'LL ALL SUFFER!

SHE MADE THEM TO RUN, TO JUMP, TO BEND UNTIL THEY COULDN'T ANYMORE. THEN MORE, THE SAME.

FOR A FEW APPELS IT WENT SO, BUT NOBODY OF ANJA'S FRIENDS GAVE HER OUT. YOU CAN IMA-GINE WHAT SHE WENT THROUGH.

66

I HAD TO STOP SENDING OVER SUCH PACKAGES MORE TO ANJA.

I LOST ANYWAY MY JOB NEAR TO HER SOON AFTER. MY WHOLE WORKSHOP THEY CLOSED OUT...

THEY PUT US BACK TO THE MAIN CAMP AND TOOK ME FOR BLACK WORK.

BLACK WORK?

CARRYING BACK AND FORTH BIG STONES, DIGGING OUT HOLES, EACH DAY DIFFERENT, BUT ALWAYS THE SAME. VERY HARD...

AND GOD FORBID, IF YOU STOPPED ONLY A MINUTE TO BREATHE.

YOU GOT A HIT TO THE HEAD, OR WORSE.

TO ME THEY NEVER HIT, BECAUSE I WORKED ALL MY MUSCLES AWAY.

I LIKED BETTER INDOORS WORK. I SOMETIMES WAS A "BETTNACH-ZIEHER"... A BED-AFTER-PULLER...

AFTER EVERYBODY FIXED THEIR BED, WE CAME TO FIX BETTER, SO THE STRAW LOOKED SQUARE.

WHAT A CRAZY JOB!

NO. THEY WANTED EVERYTHING NEAT AND IN GOOD ORDER.

BUT THESE DAYS I GOT TOO SKINNY AND IT CAME AGAIN A SELEKTION.

BLOCKSPERRE!

NOW IT COULD BE MY TURN.

RIGHT AWAY I RAN INSIDE THE TOILETS. AND IF SOMEBODY LOOKED, I'LL TELL I HAD A BAD STOMACH. WHAT HAD I TO LOSE?

NOBODY LOOKED, SO I SAT LUCKY THE WHOLE SELEKTION.

SUCH A GOOD GIRL—WITH MY SPECIAL BREAD SHE KNEW TO MAKE.... MALA WOULDN'T HAVE DONE SUCH A GOOD SANDWICH.

IT WAS THE ONLY BREAD IN THE HOUSE.

WANT SOME TEA OR COFFEE?

I CAN MAKE. I HAVE A TEA BAG NEAR TO THE SINK DRYING FROM BREAKFAST.

HOW DID YOU BE-COME A TINMAN AGAIN?

MALA COULD GO FOR A WHOLE EVENING OUT WITH HER FRIENDS AND LEAVE FOR ME NOTHING COOKED TO EAT OR DRINK.

SIGH. YOU SEE HOW IT IS? I HAVE NOW ONE MORE TIME AN UNNECESSARY SUFFERING IN MY LIFE.

SO HOW DID YOU GET BACK INTO THE TIN SHOP?

WHEN THE RUSSIANS CAME NEAR, THE GER-MANS MADE READY TO RUN FROM AUSCH-WITZ. THEY NEEDED TINMEN TO PULL APART THE MACHINERIES OF THE GAS CHAMBERS.

THEY WANTED TO PACK IT ALL TO GERMANY. THERE THEY COULD TAKE ALSO ALL OF THE JEWS TO FINISH THEM IN QUIET.

THE GERMANS DIDN'T WANT TO LEAVE ANYWHERE A SIGN OF ALL WHAT THEY DID.

YOU HEARD ABOUT THE GAS, BUT I'M TELLING NOT RUMORS, BUT ONLY WHAT REALLY I SAW.

FOR THIS I WAS AN EYEWITNESS.

I CAME TO ONE OF THE FOUR CREMO BUILDINGS. IT LOOKED SO LIKE A BIG BAKERY...

FROM BELOW GROUND, IN THE GAS ROOM, WE TINMEN HAD TO TAKE OUT THE PIPES AND FANS FOR VENTILATING.

THIS WAS A FACTORY TO MAKE —ONE, TWO, THREE— ASHES AND SMOKE FROM ALL WHAT CAME HERE.

EXE-CUTION ROOM

UNDRESS-ING ROOM

RM. FOR MELTING GOLD FILLINGS

CORPSE LIFT

GAS CHAMBER

INCINERATION RM. & OVENS

CHIMNEY

TOILET

COAL STORAGE

CREMATORIUM II.

underground undressing room

ovens

underground gas chamber

SPECIAL PRISONERS WORKED HERE SEPARATE. THEY GOT BETTER BREAD, BUT EACH FEW MONTHS THEY ALSO WERE SENT UP THE CHIMNEY. ONE FROM THEM SHOWED ME EVERYTHING HOW IT WAS.

DISINFEKTION
DEZYNFEKCIE
DISINFECTION

PEOPLE BELIEVED REALLY IT WAS HERE A PLACE FOR SHOWERS. SO THEY WERE TOLD.

THEY CAME TO A BIG ROOM TO UNDRESS THEIR CLOTHES WHAT LOOKS SO, YES-HERE IS A PLACE SO LIKE THEY SAY.

Sauber ein Ges eit

IMPORTANT REMEMBER YOUR HOOK NUMBER

PLEASE TIE YOUR SHOES TO-GETH-ER

IF I SAW A COUPLE MONTHS BEFORE HOW IT WAS ALL ARRANGED HERE, ONLY ONE TIME I COULD SEE IT!

AND EVERYBODY CROWDED INSIDE INTO THE SHOWER ROOM, THE DOOR CLOSED HERMETIC, AND THE LIGHTS TURNED DARK.

Zyklon B, a pesticide, dropped into hollow columns.

IT WAS BETWEEN 3 AND 30 MINUTES— IT DEPENDED HOW MUCH GAS THEY PUT— BUT SOON WAS NOBODY ANYMORE ALIVE.

THE BIGGEST PILE OF BODIES LAY RIGHT NEXT TO THE DOOR WHERE THEY TRIED TO GET OUT.

THIS GUY WHO WORKED THERE, HE TOLD ME...

WE PULLED THE BODIES APART WITH HOOKS. BIG PILES, WITH THE STRONGEST ON TOP, OLDER ONES AND BABIES CRUSHED BELOW... OFTEN THE SKULLS WERE SMASHED...

THEIR FINGERS WERE BROKEN FROM TRYING TO CLIMB UP THE WALLS,... AND SOMETIMES THEIR ARMS WERE AS LONG AS THEIR BODIES, PULLED FROM THE SOCKETS.

ENOUGH!

I DIDN'T WANT MORE TO HEAR, BUT ANYWAY HE TOLD ME.

THEY PULLED THE BODIES WITH AN ELEVATOR UP TO THE OVENS— MANY OVENS—AND TO EACH ONE THEY BURNED 2 OR 3 AT A TIME.

TO **SUCH** A PLACE FINISHED MY FATHER, MY SISTERS, MY BROTHERS, SO MANY

WHAT ARE THEY DOING OVER THERE—DIGGING TRENCHES IN CASE THE RUSSIANS ATTACK?

TRENCHES—HAH! THOSE ARE GIANT **GRAVES** THEY'RE FILLING IN! ...

IT STARTED IN MAY AND WENT ON ALL SUMMER. THEY BROUGHT JEWS FROM HUNGARY—TOO MANY FOR THEIR OVENS, SO THEY DUG THOSE BIG CREMATION PITS.

THE HOLES WERE BIG, SO LIKE THE SWIMMING POOL OF THE PINES HOTEL HERE.

AND TRAIN AFTER TRAIN OF HUNGARIANS CAME.

AND THOSE WHAT FINISHED IN THE GAS CHAMBERS BEFORE THEY GOT PUSHED IN THESE GRAVES, IT WAS THE **LUCKY** ONES.

THE OTHERS HAD TO JUMP IN THE GRAVES WHILE STILL THEY WERE ALIVE...

PRISONERS WHAT WORKED THERE POURED GASOLINE OVER THE LIVE ONES AND THE DEAD ONES.

AND THE FAT FROM THE BURNING BODIES THEY SCOOPED AND POURED AGAIN SO EVERYONE COULD BURN BETTER.

JESUS.

ACH! IT'S 2:30. LOOK HOW THE TIME IS FLYING. AND IT'S STILL SO MUCH TO DO TODAY...

IT'S DISHES TO CLEAN, DINNER TO DEFROST, AND MY *PILLS* I HAVEN'T YET COUNTED.

I DON'T GET IT... WHY DIDN'T THE JEWS AT LEAST *TRY* TO RESIST?

IT WASN'T SO EASY LIKE YOU THINK. EVERYONE WAS SO STARVING AND FRIGHTENED, AND TIRED THEY COULDN'T *BELIEVE* EVEN WHAT'S IN FRONT OF THEIR EYES.

...AND THE JEWS LIVED ALWAYS WITH HOPE. THEY HOPED THE RUSSIANS CAN COME BEFORE THE GERMAN BULLET ARRIVED FROM THE GUN INTO THEIR HEAD AND—

OOPS!

CRASH!

OI! YOU SEE HOW MY HEAD IS? IT'S MY FAVORITE DISH NOW BROKEN!

IT'S ONLY A *DISH*!... BUT WHY DIDN'T THEY TRY TO TAKE JUST ONE NAZI WITH THEM?

IN SOME SPOTS PEOPLE *DID* FIGHT... BUT YOU CAN KILL MAYBE ONE GERMAN BEFORE THEY KILL FAST A HUNDRED FROM YOU. THEN IT'S *EVERYONE* DEAD.

...AND THIS WAY IT WAS *ALSO* EVERYONE DEAD. NU?

DON'T THROW AWAY! I CAN GLUE STILL TOGETHER THAT PLATE.

I GUESS I'LL DO THE DISHES NOW.

NO. YOU CAN DEFROST OUT THE TURKEY LEGS.... YOU ONLY WOULD BREAK ME THE *REST* OF MY PLATES.

73

That night...

WHEW. HE'S ASLEEP AT LAST!

IT'S AMAZING HOW HARD IT IS TO SPEND A WHOLE DAY WITH HIM. HE JUST RADIATES SO MUCH TENSION.

POOR GUY. I GUESS HE'S WORSE THAN USUAL BECAUSE OF MALA...

NAH, HE'S ALWAYS THAT WAY... IT'S ONE OF THE REASONS SHE DID RUN OFF.

DO YOU THINK THEY'LL GET BACK TOGETHER?

I SURE HOPE SO. OTHERWISE HE'S OUR RESPONSIBILITY, AND I DON'T THINK I CAN TAKE HIM FOR TOO MUCH LONGER.

AAWOOWWAH!

WH-WHAT'S THAT NOISE?

OH, NOTHING— JUST VLADEK...

HE'S MOANING IN HIS SLEEP AGAIN. WHEN I WAS A KID I THOUGHT THAT WAS THE NOISE ALL GROWN-UPS MADE WHILE THEY SLEPT.

AWOO

SIGH. IT'S SO PEACEFUL HERE AT NIGHT. IT'S ALMOST IMPOSSIBLE TO BELIEVE AUSCHWITZ EVER HAPPENED.

UH-HUH. OUCH!

SLAP

BUT THESE DAMN BUGS ARE EATING ME ALIVE!

ME TOO.

PSHT

C'MON. LET'S GO INSIDE AND READ... IT'S GETTING KINDA CHILLY OUT ANYWAY.

CHAPTER THREE

I'LL PACK THE FOODS WHAT MALA LEFT TO RETURN IT OVER TO THE *SHOP-RITE*. HELP YOURSELF FOR A LITTLE CEREAL...

NO THANKS. I'LL STICK TO COFFEE.

PLEASE. JUST TASTE AND YOU'LL SEE HOW GOOD IT IS.

NO THANKS. I DON'T LIKE SPECIAL K.

BUT IT HAS *SALT* AND ALSO *SUGAR*. FOR ME IT'S *POISON* - I'LL GIVE FOR YOU A LITTLE, YES FRANÇOISE?

NO THANKS.

IT'S A SHAME TO WASTE. I'LL PACK AND YOU CAN TAKE IT HOME WITH YOU.

THE BOX IS AL-MOST EMPTY. JUST *LEAVE* IT HERE.

OKAY. IF NOT, IS NOT. ONLY JUST TRY THEN A PIECE FROM THIS FRUIT CAKE.

I'M *NOT* HUNGRY!

SO, FINE. I CAN PACK THE FRUITCAKE IN WITH THE CEREAL FOR YOU TO TAKE HOME.

LOOK. WE DON'T WANT ANY, OK? JUST FORGET IT!

I CANNOT FORGET IT... EVER SINCE HITLER I DON'T LIKE TO THROW OUT EVEN A CRUMB.

THEN JUST *SAVE* THE DAMN SPECIAL K IN CASE HITLER EVER COMES BACK!

I CAN GLUE TOGETHER THE BOX, BUT *STILL* I DON'T THINK THE SHOP-RITE WILL EXCHANGE IT!

And so...

LOOK, I'M SORRY I SNAPPED AT YOU BEFORE...

YES, THE WALLS ARE SO THIN, THE NEIGHBORS CAN HEAR EVERYTHING.

I MEAN, FRANÇOISE AND I ARE BOTH WORRIED ABOUT YOU NOW THAT MALA IS GONE, BUT YOU CAN'T EXPECT US TO MOVE IN WITH YOU PERMANENTLY...

WHAT PERMANENTLY? I WANT ONLY YOU'LL ENJOY HERE THE SUMMER WITH ME... IT'S PAID ALREADY IN FULL, WITH NO REFUND.

HOW WILL YOU MANAGE, LIVING IN REGO PARK ALL ALONE?

ALONE I CAN MANAGE MORE EASY THAN WITH MALA, BELIEVE ME.

COME. WE'LL SIT ALL THREE TOGETHER IN THE FRONT.

Y'KNOW... LAST NIGHT I WAS READING ABOUT AUSCHWITZ...

SOME PRISONERS WORKING IN THE GAS CHAMBERS REVOLTED. THEY KILLED 3 S.S. MEN AND BLEW UP A CREMATORIUM.

YAH. FOR THIS THEY ALL GOT KILLED.

AND THE FOUR YOUNG GIRLS WHAT SNEAKED OVER THE AMMUNITIONS FOR THIS, THEY HANGED THEM NEAR TO MY WORKSHOP.

THEY WERE GOOD FRIENDS OF ANJA, FROM SOSNOWIEC. THEY HANGED A LONG, LONG TIME. SIGH.

79

A COUPLE WEEKS MORE AND THEY *WOULDN'T* HANG...
IT WAS VERY NEAR TO THE END, THERE IN AUSCHWITZ.

BOOM

YOU HEAR THAT, VLADEK? THE FRONT IS NO MORE THAN 25 MILES AWAY...

IF WE CAN JUST STAY ALIVE A LITTLE BIT LONGER, THE RUSSIANS WILL BE HERE.

THIS BOY WORKED IN THE OFFICE AND KNEW RUMORS.

THE GERMANS ARE GETTING WORRIED. THE BIG SHOTS HERE ARE ALREADY RUNNING BACK INTO THE REICH.

THEY'RE PLANNING TO TAKE EVERYBODY HERE BACK TO CAMPS INSIDE GERMANY. EVERYBODY!

BUT A FEW OF US HAVE A PLAN... WE'RE NOT GOING!

!

YOU HAVE A FRIEND IN THE CAMP LAUNDRY. HELP US GET CIVILIAN CLOTHES AND JOIN US.

HE TOOK ME QUICK TO AN ATTIC IN ONE OF THE BLOCKS.

THIS ROOM ISN'T BEING USED ANYMORE. WHEN THE EVACUATION STARTS, THE SEVEN OF US WILL COME UP HERE TO HIDE.

WE ARRANGED THERE CLOTHING AND EVEN IDENTITY PAPERS, AND HALF EACH DAY'S BREAD WE PUT OVER HERE.

WE DIDN'T STAND ON THE LAST APPELS, BUT CAME UP TO THIS ATTIC.

SCREAMING GESTAPO CHASED EVERYWHERE. EACH PRISONER GOT A BREAD, A SAUSAGE AND A KICK OUT, OUT THE GATE, TO MARCH.

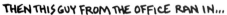

THEN THIS GUY FROM THE OFFICE RAN IN...

TERRIBLE NEWS! WE HAVE TO LEAVE!

THEY'RE GOING TO SET FIRE TO THE CAMP AND BOMB ALL THE BLOCKS! HURRY!

FINALLY THEY *DIDN'T* BOMB, BUT THIS WE COULDN'T KNOW. WE LEFT BEHIND EVERY-THING, WE WERE SO AFRAID, EVEN THE CIVILIAN CLOTHES WE ORGANIZED. AND RAN OUT!

IT WAS ALREADY NIGHT, THEY GAVE TO EACH OF US A BLANKET AND A LITTLE BIT FOOD TO CARRY, AND WE WENT OUT FROM AUSCHWITZ, MAYBE THE LAST ONE.

ALL NIGHT I HEARD SHOOTING. HE WHO GOT TIRED, WHO CAN'T WALK SO FAST, THEY SHOT.

THE MORE WE WALKED, THE MORE I HEARD SHOOTING...

AND IN THE DAYLIGHT, FAR AHEAD, I SAW IT.

KRAK

SOMEBODY IS JUMPING, TURNING, ROLLING 25 OR 35 TIMES AROUND. AND STOPS.

"OH," I SAID. "THEY MAYBE KILLED THERE A DOG."

WHEN I WAS A BOY OUR NEIGHBOR HAD A DOG WHAT GOT MAD AND WAS BITING.

KPOW

THE NEIGHBOR CAME OUT WITH A RIFLE AND SHOT.

THE DOG WAS ROLLING SO, AROUND AND AROUND, KICKING, BEFORE HE LAY QUIET.

AND NOW I THOUGHT: "HOW AMAZING IT IS THAT A HUMAN BEING REACTS THE SAME LIKE THIS NEIGHBOR'S DOG."

ONE OF THE BOYS WHAT WE WERE IN THE ATTIC TOGETHER, TALKED OVER TO THE GUARD...

PSST_LOOK. THE WAR IS ALMOST OVER. SOME OF US WANT TO ESCAPE INTO THE WOODS. WE CAN PAY...

?

SHARE THIS GOLD WITH THE GUARDS IN FRONT AND BEHIND. JUST DON'T SHOOT WHEN WE RUN...

WE'LL GIVE YOU THE SIGNAL LATE TO-NIGHT, AND SHOOT OVER YOUR HEADS.

ALL DAY LONG THEY WERE ARRANGING...

IT'S ALL SET, VLADEK. HELP PAY OFF THE GUARDS AND JOIN US.

ACH. HOW CAN YOU TRUST THE GERMANS?!

AT NIGHT WAS A COMMOTION. 8 OR 9 RAN OFF...

BANG

AND OF COURSE YOU COULDN'T TRUST...

SO THE MARCH WAS GOING AND GOING. FOREVER WE MARCHED. AND THE ONES WHAT DIDN'T FALL DOWN, WE MARCHED.

AND SO WE CAME OVER TO GROSS-ROSEN.

HERE WAS A SMALL CAMP, WITH NO GAS.

IT WAS THOUSANDS OF PRISONERS FROM ALL AROUND BEING PULLED BACK INTO GERMANY.

EVERYWHERE WAS CONFUSION AND HITTING. TERRIBLE!

YOU SHITS OVER THERE! GO HAUL THE SOUP FROM THE KITCHEN—TWO TO EACH PAIL.

THEY CAUGHT 20 OF US TO CARRY.

YOU SEE WHAT'S GOING ON HERE. STAY WITH ME!

I GRABBED FAST A GUY WHAT WAS STILL STRONG LIKE ME.

MOST COULDN'T EVEN LIFT THEY WERE WEAK FROM MARCHING AND NO FOOD.

QUICK! QUICK!

BEHIND I HEARD YELLING AND SHOUTING. I DIDN'T LOOK.

LAZY BASTARDS! LOOK AT HOW THOSE TWO RUN!

WE GOT AN EXTRA PORTION SOUP FOR THIS. MOST WERE NOT LUCKY TO BE STILL STRONG.

IN THE MORNING THEY CHASED US TO MARCH AGAIN OUT, WHO KNOWS WHERE...

THROUGH THE TOWN WE WERE GOING. IT WAS EMPTY, WITH NO PRIVATE PEOPLE. AND WE SAW, FROM FAR, A TRAIN.

IT WAS SUCH A TRAIN FOR HORSES, FOR COWS.

INSIDE! MOVE! MOVE!

THEY PUSHED UNTIL IT WAS NO ROOM LEFT.

WE LAY ONE ON TOP THE OTHER, LIKE MATCHES, LIKE HERRINGS,

I PUSHED TO A CORNER NOT TO GET CRUSHED...

HIGH UP I SAW A FEW HOOKS TO CHAIN UP MAYBE THE ANIMALS.

I HAD STILL THE THIN BLANKET THEY GAVE ME,

I CLIMBED TO SOME-BODY'S SHOULDER AND HOOKED IT STRONG.

IN THIS WAY I CAN REST AND BREATHE A LITTLE.

THIS SAVED ME. MAY-BE 25 PEOPLE CAME OUT FROM THIS CAR OF 200.

SO, THE TRAIN WAS GOING, WE DIDN'T KNOW WHERE.

AND THEN IT **STOPPED.**

FOR DAYS AND NIGHTS, NOTHING

NO FOOD AND NO WATER, ONLY SCREAMS INSIDE.

YOU SEE, PEOPLE BEGAN TO DIE, TO FAINT...

AI! MY LEGS! I'M BEING STABBED!

AII!

IT WASN'T **ROOM** TO FALL ...AND IF HE FELL, THEY STOOD ON HIM.

SO HE JABBED TO THEIR LEGS WITH A KNIFE, BUT USUALLY HE ANYWAY DIED.

IF SOMEONE HAD TO MAKE A VRINE OR A BOWEL MOVEMENT, HE DID WHERE HE STOOD.

IF HE HAD STILL FOOD, HE ATE IT.

I ATE MOSTLY SNOW FROM UP ON THE ROOF.

SOME HAD SUGAR SOMEHOW, BUT IT BURNED.

MY THROAT! I NEED WATER! WATER! GIVE ME SOME SNOW!

I CAN ONLY REACH A LITTLE FOR MYSELF!

PLEASE! PLEASE!! I BEG YOU!

OKAY. GIVE ME SOME SUGAR, I'LL GET YOU SOME SNOW...

SO I ATE ALSO SUGAR AND SAVED THEIR LIFE.

THE TRAIN STAYED SO, WITHOUT MOVING, I DON'T KNOW HOW LONG, UP TO A WEEK...

THEN, ONE DAY THEY OPENED...

THROW OUT THE DEAD, AND CLEAN UP YOUR FILTH!

IF THE DEAD HAD BREAD LEFT, OR BETTER SHOES, WE KEPT...

OUTSIDE WERE MANY TRAINS STANDING FOR WEEKS, WHAT THEY *NEVER* OPENED, AND IT WAS EVERYONE DEAD INSIDE...

...THEY DIDN'T NEED ANYMORE.

THEY CLOSED US AGAIN. WE WERE VERY HAPPY WE HAD NOW ROOM WHERE TO STAND.

NEAR TO THE DOOR WE PILED NEW DEAD ONES. EACH DAY THE GERMANS OPENED: "HOW MANY DEAD?" AND WE THREW OUT, AND SOON WE HAD ROOM EVEN TO SIT.

THEN THE TRAIN STARTED AGAIN GOING AND GOING... INSIDE WE WERE MORE DYING AND SOME GOT CRAZY.

THEY OPENED THAT WE WILL THROW OUT THE DEAD...

WE'VE GOTTA GET OUT! LET US OUT! OUT! OUT!

THEN AGAIN IT STOPPED.

ALL OF YOU—GET DOWN!

WE COULD NOT BELIEVE WHAT WE ARE SEEING!

YES! AND THE GIRLS ARE GIVING TO EVERYBODY A SNACK—A LITTLE COFFEE AND A PIECE OF BREAD...

THERE IS THE RED CROSS!...

WE DIDN'T REMEMBER EVEN HOW BREAD LOOKS. WE WERE VERY HAPPY.

THEN THEY CHASED US BACK IN THE TRAIN AGAIN TO DIE, AND SO THE TRAVEL CONTINUED MORE...

IN THE MIDDLE WE FOUND OUT THAT WE ARE COMING TO DACHAU.

FROM ALL THE CAMPS OF EUROPE THEY NOW BROUGHT BACK ALL OF US INSIDE GERMANY.

THIS WAS EARLY FEBRUARY, IN 1945. IT WAS NO FOOD AND SO CROWDED—

LOOK WHERE YOU GO!

ACH! THE SHOP-RITE IS *THERE*, AND YOU DIDN'T TURN TO IT!

WHOOSH

SO, COME. WE'LL GO NOW IN TO GIVE BACK OUR GROCERIES.

NO WAY! I'M NOT GOING IN TO RETURN A LOAD OF OPEN BOXES AND PARTIALLY EATEN FOOD.

WHAT'S TO BE SO ASHAMED? IT'S FOODS I CAN'T EAT. YOU WAIT THEN IN THE CAR WHILE *I* ARRANGE IT.

Y'KNOW... I'LL BET YOU THAT ANJA'S NOTEBOOKS WERE WRITTEN ON BOTH SIDES OF THE PAGE...

HUH? I CAN'T REMEMBER. WHY D'YOU SAY THAT?

WELL... IF THERE WERE ANY *BLANK* PAGES VLADEK WOULD NEVER HAVE BURNED THEM.

UH HUH... HEY! YOU CAN SEE HIM IN THE WINDOW!

JEEZ. VLADEK AND THE MANAGER ARE *SHOUTING* AT EACH OTHER...

NOW THE MANAGER IS JUST WALKING AWAY FROM HIM...

AND NOW VLADEK IS TRAILING AFTER HIM...

HOW EMBARRASSING.

SIGH. I'D RATHER KILL MYSELF THAN LIVE THROUGH ALL THAT...

WHAT? RETURNING GROCERIES?

NO. EVERYTHING VLADEK WENT THROUGH. IT'S A MIRACLE HE SURVIVED.

UH-HUH. BUT IN SOME WAYS HE DIDN'T SURVIVE.

MAYBE WE SHOULD STAY WITH HIM A FEW DAYS LONGER. HE NEEDS HELP.

ARE YOU KIDDING?

...I DON'T THINK WE'D SURVIVE.

YOO-HOO!

YOU SEE? I EXCHANGED AND GOT SIX DOLLARS WORTH OF NEW GROCERIES FOR ONLY ONE DOLLAR!

INCREDIBLE!...

...WE WERE SURE YOU'D GET KICKED OUT OF THE STORE!

WHAT ARE YOU TALKING? THE MANAGER IS A VERY FINE GENTLEMAN...

HE HELPED ME AS SOON I EXPLAINED TO HIM MY HEALTH, HOW MALA LEFT ME, AND HOW IT WAS IN THE CAMPS.

OY! GET IN... WE CAN'T EVER SHOW OUR FACES HERE AGAIN.

NOW WE'LL DRIVE BACK SO I CAN PHONE TO MY LAWYER ON MALA.

DACHAU... YOU WERE SAYING IT WAS VERY CROWDED IN THAT CAMP...

YAH-THIS WAS A CAMP-*TERRIBLE!* I HAD A MISERY, I CAN'T TELL YOU... HERE, IN DACHAU, MY TROUBLES BEGAN.

WE WERE CLOSED IN BARRACKS, SITTING ON STRAW, WAITING ONLY TO DIE.

IN THE STRAW, IT WAS LICE...

FROM THE LICE WAS TYPHUS.

TO EAT WE GOT ONLY BREAD AND SOUP, BUT YOU HAD TO SHOW FIRST YOUR SHIRT...

IF IT WAS ANY LICE, YOU GOT NO SOUP. THIS WAS IMPOSSIBLE. *EVERYWHERE* WAS LICE!

AND, GOD FORBID, IF SOMEONE GOT SOUP AND SOMEONE *SPILLED* HIM A DROP...

LIKE WILD ANIMALS THEY WOULD FIGHT UNTIL THERE WAS BLOOD.

YOU CAN'T KNOW WHAT IT IS, TO BE HUNGRY.

91

THERE, IN DACHAU, I GOT AN INFECTION IN MY HAND...

I TRIED TO MAKE WORSE AND WORSE MY INFECTION...

I WANTED THEY TAKE ME TO THE INFIRMARY.

EACH FEW DAYS SOMEONE CAME TO SEE WHO IS SICK...

GO WITH THEM...

YOU SEE, THE INFIRMARY, I HEARD IT WAS A PARADISE.

PUT THIS OINTMENT ON HIS HAND AND KEEP IT BANDAGED. IT WILL CLEAR UP QUICKLY.

HERE I HAD THREE TIMES A DAY SOMETHING TO EAT, AND IT WAS ONLY TWO PATIENTS FOR EACH BED.

I WORKED HOW I COULD WITH ONE HAND, SO THEY WILL LIKE ME.

THAT'S STRANGE, IT SHOULD HAVE HEALED BY NOW!

I IRRITATED EACH DAY MY HAND, TO STAY LONGER.

AII!

THERE! I OPENED IT UP AGAIN!

THIS HURT ME REALLY VERY VERY MUCH...

I GOT AFRAID FOR MY HAND AND LET IT HEAL.

...I HAVE STILL TODAY A SCAR ON THIS PLACE.

FROM THE INFIRMARY I HAD TO GO BACK TO A BAD BARRACK, WHERE WE WERE ALL DAY STANDING OUTSIDE.

PARLEZ-VOUS FRANÇAIS?

WHA? NO...

IT WAS NOTHING TO EAT, AND NOTHING TO DO, ONLY TO WAIT AND TO DIE.

I CAN SPEAK GERMAN, YIDDISH, POLISH AND ENGLISH.

ANGLAIS?!

DIEU MERCI! I TALK ENGLISH ALSO A LITTLE. I WAS BECOMING CRAZY!...

THERE IS NO OTHER FRENCH HERE AND I DO NOT KNOW TO TALK GERMAN. I HAD NOBODY TO WHO TO TALK.

YOU ARE A POLE-JEW, YES? HOW YOU KNOW ENGLISH?

ACCH... I DREAMED ALWAYS TO GO ONE DAY TO AMERICA.

SO, WE TALKED, AND IT MADE THE TIME LIGHTER.

EACH DAY HE FOUND ME, THE FRENCH MAN...

BRR. GOOD MORNING. IT IS AGAIN VERY COLD TODAY.

LOOK TO THIS, MY FRIEND. I HAVE A **BOX**!

HE WAS NOT A JEW, SO BY THE RED CROSS THEY LET PACKAGES COME TO HIM.

MY FAMILY SENDS. I WANT THAT YOU ALSO EAT SOMETHING.

MY GOD. SARDINES! BISCUITS! CHOCOLATE!

HE INSISTED TO SHARE WITH ME, AND IT SAVED ME MY LIFE.

93

WITH MY NEW FOOD I CAME TO AN IDEA...

PSST- DO YOU WANT TO BUY A BAR OF CHOCOLATE?

CHOCOLATE?! DO I LOOK LIKE A MILLIONAIRE?

I'LL TRADE IT FOR YOUR SHIRT.

MY SHIRT?! YOU'RE CRAZY-I'D FREEZE!

UM-GIVE ME YOUR DAY'S RATION OF BREAD TOO.

IN AUSCHWITZ A SHIRT WAS NOT SO EXPENSIVE, BUT HERE NO GOODS CAME IN.

I CLEANED THE SHIRT VERY, VERY CAREFUL.

AND OUTSIDE, I DRIED IT.

I WAS LUCKY TO FIND A PIECE OF PAPER...

SO, CAREFUL I WRAPPED IT.

I UNWRAPPED ONLY WHEN THEY CALLED TO SOUP...

HERE WAS A SHIRT WITH REALLY NO LICE!

MY OLD SHIRT I HID TO MY PANTS. I SHOWED THE NEW ONE.

OKAY.

RIGHT AWAY THEY GAVE ME TO EAT.

YOU ARE A GENIUS, VLADEK. A GENIUS!

I HELPED THE FRENCHMAN TO ALSO ORGANIZE A SHIRT, SO WE BOTH GOT ALWAYS SOUP.

94

BUT AFTER A FEW WEEKS I GOT TOO SICK EVEN TO EAT...

TYPHUS!

I GOT VERY HOT FEVER AND I COULDN'T SLEEP. **TYPHUS!**

EVERY NIGHT PEOPLE DIED OF THIS.

AT NIGHT I HAD TO GO TO THE TOILET DOWN. IT WAS ALWAYS FULL, THE WHOLE CORRIDOR, WITH THE DEAD PEOPLE PILED THERE. YOU COULDN'T GO THROUGH...

YOU HAD TO GO ON THEIR HEADS, AND THIS WAS TERRIBLE, BECAUSE IT WAS SO SLIPPERY, THE SKIN, YOU THOUGHT YOU ARE FALLING. AND THIS WAS EVERY NIGHT.

SO NOW I HAD TYPHUS, AND I HAD TO GO TO THE TOILET DOWN, AND I SAID, "NOW IT'S **MY** TIME. NOW I WILL BE LAYING LIKE THIS ONES AND SOMEBODY WILL STEP ON ME!"

I WAS ALIVE STILL THE NEXT TIME IT CAME A GUY FROM THE INFIRMARY...

MANY DIDN'T LIVE LONG ENOUGH TO GO TO DIE IN THE INFIRMARY.

THERE I LAY TOO WEAK EVEN TO MOVE OR TO GO TO THE TOILET OUT FROM BED.

I ASKED HELP FROM THE FELLOWS NEXT TO ME, BUT IN A FEW HOURS THEY WERE DEAD AND OTHERS CAME.

THEY GAVE BREAD AND SOUP, BUT I WAS TOO WEAK TO EAT...

SO I PUT MY PORTION BELOW MY PILLOW.

HEY! THERE'S STALE BREAD ALL OVER THIS ONE'S BED!

WELL, TAKE IT AWAY... HE'LL NEVER NEED IT.

I SCREAMED. BUT I **COULDN'T** SCREAM.

MMUH MMNH.

I WAS TOO **WEAK** TO SCREAM...

SO I TOOK MY SHOE AND KNOCKED LOUD.

KLAKK KLAKK KLAKK

STOP THAT RACKET!

BAH! KEEP YOUR DAMN BREAD!

I COULDN'T EAT, BUT I CUT PIECES TO PAY FOR HELP TO GO DOWN TO THE TOILET.

SO... MY FEVER FELL DOWN, AND SOMETHING NEW CAME.

ATTENTION!...

EVERYONE STRONG ENOUGH TO TRAVEL, LINE UP OUTSIDE....

YOU WILL BE EXCHANGED AS WAR PRISONERS AT THE SWISS BORDER.

WAS I DREAMING ONLY?!

THEY LIKED TO SEND OUT THE SICK ONES, BUT NOT SO SICK THAT WE ARRIVE DEAD.

I WAS VERY WEAK, BUT, FOR MY BREAD I HAD TWO FRIENDS WHAT HELPED ME.

WHEN THEY LEFT ME GO FOR EVEN A SECOND, MY LEGS DIDN'T HOLD ME.

BUT I CAME SOMEHOW OUTSIDE THE GATE...

GASP! A TRAIN!

HERE WAS A TRAIN NOT FOR COWS AND HORSES, BUT A REAL TRAIN TO TAKE PASSENGERS—A TRAIN FOR PEOPLE!

I THOUGHT THIS TRAIN, IT MUST BE FOR THE *GESTAPO*, BUT **NO!**

IT TOOK US OUT FROM DACHAU, IN THE DIRECTION TO SWITZERLAND.

WHATEVER HAPPENED TO THAT FRENCH GUY WHO HELPED YOU?

YAH. HE WAS A FINE FELLOW...

I CAN'T REMEMBER EVEN HIS NAME, BUT IN PARIS HE IS LIVING.... FOR YEARS WE EXCHANGED LETTERS IN THE ENGLISH I TAUGHT TO HIM.

WELL...DID YOU SAVE ANY OF HIS LETTERS?

OF COURSE I SAVED. BUT ALL THIS I THREW AWAY TOGETHER WITH ANJA'S NOTEBOOKS.

ALL SUCH THINGS OF THE WAR, I TRIED TO PUT OUT FROM MY MIND ONCE FOR ALL... UNTIL YOU *REBUILD* ME ALL THIS FROM YOUR QUESTIONS.

?!

HAH?! WHAT FOR DO YOU STOP, FRANÇOISE? WE'RE NOT YET TO THE BUNGALOW?

THERE'S A HITCH-HIKER...

SKREEEEEK!

A HITCH-HIKER? AND -OY- IT'S A *COLORED GUY, A SHVARTSER!*

HIYA.

PUSH QUICK ON THE GAS!

THANKS. IT'S A HOT DAY FO' WALKIN'.

MÓZ BOŻE! CO SIĘ STAŁO JEGO ŻONIE? CZY ONA ZGŁUPIAŁA?*

*(POLISH:) Oh my God! What's happened to his wife? She's lost her **head**!!

MAH COUSIN'S PLACE IS JUS' UP TH' ROAD.

PSIA KREW! CHOLERA! TO NIE MOŻLIWE. A SHVARTSER SIEDZI TU ZE MNĄ! *

*(POLISH:) ⊙!★!! I just can't believe it! There's a **SHVARTSER** sitting in here!

Y'ALL TAKE CARE NOW, AN' BE GOOD.

WHAT **HAPPENED** ON YOU, FRANÇOISE? YOU WENT CRAZY, OR WHAT?!

I HAD THE WHOLE TIME TO WATCH OUT THAT THIS **SHVARTSER** DOESN'T STEAL US THE GROCERIES FROM THE BACK SEAT!

WHAT?!

THAT'S **OUTRAGEOUS!** HOW CAN YOU, OF ALL PEOPLE, BE SUCH A RACIST! YOU TALK ABOUT BLACKS THE WAY THE NAZIS TALKED ABOUT THE JEWS!

ACH!...

I THOUGHT REALLY YOU ARE MORE SMART THAN THIS, FRANÇOISE...

IT'S NOT EVEN TO **COMPARE**, THE SHVARTSERS AND THE JEWS!

BUT HOW *DARE* YOU GENERALIZE AND SAY ALL BLACKS STEAL! IT'S

JUST STOP, YES? YOU ONLY DON'T *KNOW* THEM...

WHEN FIRST I CAME TO NEW YORK I WORKED IN THE GARMENT CENTER. BEFORE THIS I DIDN'T *SEE* COLOREDS...

BUT THERE IT WAS SHVARTSERS EVERYWHERE, AND IF I PUT DOWN ONLY FOR ONE SECOND MY VALUABLES, THEY TOOK!

BUT, YOU—

FORGET IT, HONEY... HE'S HOPELESS.

YAH!...

BETTER WE'LL JUST *FORGET* IT.

AH!... YOU SEE, KIDS... WE'RE HOME SWEET HOME ALREADY...

...NOW WE CAN MAKE A VERY HAPPY LUNCH FROM ALL MY NEW GROCERIES.

ONLY THANK GOD THAT YOUR *SHVARTSER* DIDN'T TAKE THEM.

COS
BU
B

COSMO
BUNG
COLO

Back in Rego Park. Late Autumn...

ALWAYS I SAVED...

I SAVED ONLY SO I CAN HAVE A LITTLE SOMETHING FOR MY OLD AGE.

SO, NOW I HAVE MY OLD AGE, AND *LOOK* WHAT I HAVE ...

I HAVE A TANK WITH OXYGEN AND I'M SO WEAK WITH MY HEART AND MY DIABETES, I CAN'T LIVE ANYMORE ALONE

I HAVE SO MUCH *ROOM.* YOU AND FRANÇOISE CAN COME AND, FOR NO RENT, LIVE HERE BY ME ...

NO! THAT'S TOTALLY OUT OF THE QUESTION.

SO, HOW HAVE I TO LIVE, ARTIE... TELL ME! TO GO TO A *RETIRING* HOME, IT'S NOT FOR ME.

WELL, WHY NOT GET A LIVE-IN NURSE? YOU CAN AFFORD IT.

AND WHAT WILL MY *NEIGHBORS* SAY TO IT IF THEY SEE A WOMAN IS LIVING BY ME!

WHA?? SO HIRE A *MALE* NURSE!

YAH! YOU AND MALA, YOU DON'T KNOW TO *MAKE* MONEY, ONLY TO MAKE IT *DISAPPEAR!*

IF I GIVE ON MALA $100,000 OVER TO HER NAME, *THEN* SHE'LL LIVE AGAIN HERE. *THIS* YOU ADVISE ME?

IT'S UP TO YOU.

I ONLY DON'T KNOW HOW TO ARRANGE MYSELF... MAYBE TO YOUR ROOM I CAN FIND A TENANT TO TAKE CARE ON ME.

UH-HUH. MAY-BE...

WELL... COME! WE HAVE NOW TO CARRY UP MY STORM WINDOWS TO PUT IN.

SHIT. I WAS HOPING YOU'D TELL ME MORE OF YOUR STORY...

THIS WE CAN TALK MAYBE AFTER, BUT ALREADY I'M COLD. I LOSE MONEY TO HEAT WITH NO STORM WINDOWS.

SIGH.

IN OTHER YEARS I PUT BY NOW THE WINDOWS, THAT I DIDN'T NEED HELP.

LOOK... I'LL DO IT, BUT FIRST, JUST TELL ME MORE ABOUT ANJA.

ANJA? WHAT IS TO TELL? EVERYWHERE I LOOK I'M SEEING ANJA...

FROM MY GOOD EYE, FROM MY GLASS EYE, IF THEY'RE OPEN OR THEY'RE CLOSED, ALWAYS I'M THINKING ON ANJA.

UH, I MEANT WHEN YOU WERE IN DACHAU. WHERE WAS ANJA?

ZZIK

I DON'T KNOW—TO DIFFERENT CAMPS... SHE MARCHED FROM AUSCHWITZ EARLIER AS ME, AND CAME ALSO THROUGH GROSS-ROSEN, AND THEN—I DON'T REMEMBER—

103

BUT HOW DID ANJA SURVIVE?

MANCIE-THE HUNGARIAN GIRL WHAT I KNEW THERE IN AUSCHWITZ-SHE KEPT ANJA CLOSE BY TO HER.

AFTER THE WAR I LOOKED ALWAYS FOR MANCIE, TO GIVE A NICE RE-WARD, BUT I DIDN'T KNOW EVEN HER FULL NAME, AND I NEVER FOUND!

MOM USED TO MENTION RAVENSBRÜCK. WAS MANCIE WITH HER THERE?

YAH... MAYBE IT WAS THERE...

I KNOW ONLY THAT ANJA CAME OUT FREE BY THE RUSSIAN SIDE AND SHE CAME BACK TO SOSNOWIEC BEFORE ME. MY LIBERATION, IT TOOK LONGER...

IT WAS THE LAST MINUTES OF THE WAR, I LEFT DACHAU...

I WENT TO BE EX-CHANGED FOR GER-MAN PRISONERS ON THE SWISS BORDER BUT WE NEVER CAME.

I REMEMBER WE GOT EACH A TREASURE BOX FROM THE SWISS RED CROSS: SARDINES! BISCUITS! CHOCOLATE!

SOME ATE RIGHT AWAY EVERYTHING. I KEPT, OF COURSE, TO HAVE LATER.

SO, AT NIGHT, SOME TRIED TO STEAL FROM ME...

HEY!

WITH MY TYPHUS I NEEDED STILL MUCH TO REST, BUT THIS TREASURE WAS MORE TO ME THAN SLEEPING.

EVERYBODY OUT! LINE UP IN FIVES!

HERE WAS THE END OF OUR RIDE.

WE HAD FROM HERE TO GO BY FOOT TO THE FRONTIER...

AND I SAW, IT'S NOT EVERYWHERE, MY HELL. IT'S STILL **LIFE** THINGS GOING ON.

WE MARCH. WE STOP. FOR **HOURS** WE STOOD.

(WHAT'S GOING ON?)

(THEY'RE TAKING US BACK TO DACHAU!)

(NO, NO. THE AMERICANS ARE COMING.)

IT WAS COMMOTIONS AND RUMORS, THEN SHOUTS:

THE WAR IS OVER!

IT WAS OVER.

MARCH BACK TO THE TRACKS! **SCHNELL!**

THEY DIDN'T LEAVE US GO, BUT PUT US TO A FREIGHT TRAIN.

THE AMERICANS WILL BE IN THE NEXT TOWN. THEY CAN HAVE YOU.

ON THIS TRAIN NO GUARDS CAME. SO REALLY WE SAW, IT IS OVER NOW.

IN A HALF HOUR THIS TRAIN STOPPED

HEY! THE AMERICANS AREN'T HERE!

WHY WAIT? LET'S GO!

SOME WENT ONE WAY, SOME ANOTHER...

WE DIDN'T KNOW *WHERE* WE WENT.

HALT OR WE'LL SHOOT!

ALL OF A SUDDEN, IT WAS A WEHRMACHT PATROL!

LITTLE BY LITTLE THEY GOT ALL OF US WHAT WERE GOING TO BE FREE, MAYBE 150 OR 200 PEOPLE OVER IN THE WOODS, BY A BIG LAKE !!!

I DIDN'T UNDERSTAND WHAT IS GOING ON, BUT I WAS AGAIN HERE IN GERMAN HANDS.

THEY GUARDED SO WE COULDN'T GO AWAY.

THERE ARE MACHINE GUNS SET UP ALL AROUND US!

WE OVERHEARD. THEY INTEND TO MURDER EVERY ONE OF US TONIGHT, RIGHT ON THIS SPOT!

IN THE LATER AFTERNOON I WENT OVER CLOSE TO THE EDGE OF THE WATER ...

VLADEK SPIEGELMAN! IS THAT YOU?!

SHIVEK?! YOU'RE ALIVE?

SHIVEK WAS FROM BEFORE THE WAR. A FRIEND FROM BEDZIN, NEAR SOSNOWIEC.

WE SURVIVED EVERYTHING JUST TO GET SHOT WHILE THE WAR ENDS!

I STILL HAVE A LITTLE COFFEE I ORGANIZED. LET'S MAKE A LAST CUP.

LOOK! GET HIM!

SPLASH

ONE OLDER GUY, HE WAS MAYBE 50, JUMPED TO THE LAKE. IT WAS A FAR SWIM.

KBANG! KBANG!

HE MADE IT! DO YOU HAVE THE STRENGTH TO TRY?

JUST STAY NEAR THE WATER. WE CAN ALWAYS TRY IT WHEN THE REAL SHOOTING STARTS.

SO IT CAME NIGHT. WE WERE TERRIBLE FRIGHTENED. WE SAT AND WAITED.

IT WAS CRYING AND PRAYING. SO LONG WE SURVIVED, AND NOW WE WAITED ONLY THAT THEY SHOOT, BECAUSE WE HAD NOT ELSE TO DO.

WE HEARD ALL NIGHT SHOOTING IN THE MOUNTAINS AROUND...

KPOK KPOK KPOK

OUR GUARDS- THEY ALL RAN AWAY!

SO THIS NEXT MORNING WE WERE *STILL* AGAIN ALIVE!

COME, SHIVEK. LET'S FIND A BUNKER UNTIL THINGS QUIET DOWN.

WE CAME BY A GARAGE. SO I WENT OVER...

PLEASE, SIR. WE NEED A PLACE TO HIDE 'TIL THE AMERICANS GET HERE.

GO AWAY! I DON'T WANT TO GET IN-VOLVED!

HAVE PITY. IT'S JUST FOR A DAY OR TWO!...

WELL...THERE'S A *PIT* IN THE BACK. IT'S NONE OF *MY* BUSINESS IF YOU WANT TO LIE IN IT!

OVER A DAY WE LAY THERE. THEN TWO WEHRMACHT CAME.

HEY! WHICH WAY IS INNSBRUCK?

THAT WAY, OFFICER.

BUT *WAIT*-TWO JEWS ARE BACK THERE, HIDING IN A PIT!

THEY WERE IN SO BIG A HURRY TO *RUN*, THEY DIDN'T EVEN *LOOK* TO US.

109

LET'S GO, SHIVEK. WE'LL FIND A SAFER SPOT.

WE PASSED TO A FEW HOUSES AND PEEKED INSIDE...

LOOK. NOBODY SEEMS TO BE HOME HERE.

A PART OF THIS HOUSE, IT WAS A BARN.

WE CAN HIDE UP HERE UNDER THE HAY.

FROM THE WALLS WE HEARD SHOUTING:

SCHNELL, ELSA! PACK WHAT YOU CAN.

HURRY! THIS MAY BECOME A BATTLEFIELD ANY MINUTE!

KKABOOMM

THE VILLAGERS ARE RUNNING AWAY!

FINE. THE FARTHER THE BETTER!

THE FAR SIDE FROM OUR BARN FELL DOWN A LITTLE...

MY GOD! WH-WHAT HAPPENED?!

THE WEHRMACHT IS RETREATING AND BLEW UP THE BRIDGE TO SEAL THEIR TRAIL. IT MEANS WE'RE FREE!

LET'S LOOK AROUND. IT'S SAFE NOW!

UH-UH. I'M NOT GOING ANYWHERE!

I WENT MYSELF TO THE EMPTY HOUSE.

GASP. MILK!

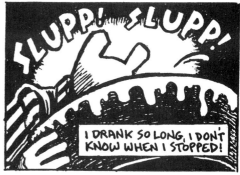

SLUPP! SLUPP!

I DRANK SO LONG, I DON'T KNOW WHEN I STOPPED!

I TOLD YOU IT'S SAFE NOW. I GOT YOU SOME MILK!

MILK!

SO, WE BOTH DRANK TOO MUCH MILK AND LOOKED AROUND.

AAH! CHICKENS!

HE WAS A FARM BOY, SHIVEK. HE KILLED EACH DAY A CHICKEN, AND MILKED US A COW.

I USED TO DREAM ABOUT CHICKENS!

SKRAAAK!

LOOK! I FOUND CLOTHES UPSTAIRS. WE CAN THROW AWAY OUR STRIPES.

THERE! I'M STARTING TO FEEL HUMAN AGAIN!

ME TOO. EXCEPT I'M -ULP GETTING N-NAUSEOUS...

WE LAY A FEW DAYS IN BAD SHAPE UNTIL THE AMERICANS CAME...

HANDS UP! IDENTIFY YOURSELVES!

OUR STOMACH GOT A SHOCK TO EAT MILK AND CHICKENS. WE GOT VERY SICK OF DIARRHEA.

111

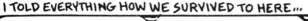
I TOLD EVERYTHING HOW WE SURVIVED TO HERE...

...AND FROM DACHAU WE CAME OVER BY TRAIN TO— AII!

BANG BANG BANG!

THAT'S JUST MY MEN SIGNALING THAT THEY FOUND A CACHE OF GERMAN AMMO...

THOSE KRAUTS CAN'T HURT YOU ANYMORE. THE ONLY ONES LEFT ARE DEAD OR DYING.

THIS HOUSE WILL BE PART OF OUR BASE CAMP...

BUT I GUESS YOU BOYS CAN STAY IF YOU KEEP THE JOINT CLEAN AND MAKE OUR BEDS.

WANT SOME CHOCOLATE?

M-MAYBE FOR LATER. THANK YOU.

SO WE WORKED FOR THE AMERICANS AND THEY LIKED ME THAT I CAN SPEAK ENGLISH.

THANKS FOR THE SHINE, WILLIE.

IT'S OKAY, SERGEANT. DON'T EVEN MENTION.

THEY GAVE TO US FOOD CANS AND GIFTS AND CALLED TO ME "WILLIE."

ONE TIME IT CAME A WOMAN WITH *OFFICIALS* TO THE HOUSE.

ARREST THOSE TWO JEWISH THIEVES!

THEY STOLE MY HUSBAND'S CLOTHES!

WE NEVER *LOOKED* ON WHAT CLOTHES WE TOOK!

ROB-BERS!

YOU'LL HAVE TO GIVE 'EM BACK, WILLIE.

"SO, LET HER TAKE," I TOLD. "WE HAVE *STILL* 3 FULL VALISES!"

ACH! LOOK ON THE TIME! WE HAVE TO *HURRY* NOW WITH MY WINDOWS.

BUT, BEFORE I FORGET— I PUT HERE A BOX WHAT YOU'LL BE HAPPY TO SEE.

I THOUGHT I LOST IT, BUT YOU SEE HOW I SAVED!

MOM'S DIA-RIES?!

NO, NO! ON THOSE IT'S NO MORE TO SPEAK. THOSE IT'S GONE, *FINISHED!*

BUT, BELOW MY CLOSET I FIND THESE SNAPSHOTS, SOME STILL FROM POLAND.

THANKS.

COME. YOU'LL LOOK *AFTER* THE WINDOWS!

IS THIS UNCLE HERMAN?

THESE PHOTOS WE GOT FROM RICHIEU'S POLISH GOVERNESS.

WE GAVE HER OUR VALUABLE THINGS TO HOLD UNTIL THE WAR IS OVER.

BUT AFTERWARD SHE SAID, "ALL THESE VALUABLES, THE NAZIS GRABBED AWAY."

WE DIDN'T BELIEVE, BUT THE PICTURES AT LEAST, SHE GAVE BACK.

CAN I TAKE THESE HOME?

YAH. IT'S FOR YOU. BUT, WAIT— I'LL PUT THEM TO AN ENVELOPE...

THE CIGAR BOX I CAN NEED FOR— AKKH!

WHOO-YOU SEE! MY NITRO-STAT HELPS ME RIGHT AWAY. BUT I TALKED TOO MUCH. I'LL LIE A LITTLE DOWN.

UM—WHAT ABOUT THE STORM WINDOWS?

ALONE YOU CAN'T KNOW HOW TO DO, AND I'M NOW TOO TIRED FOR THIS. MAYBE TOMORROW WE'LL DO.

IMPOSSIBLE. I'M TOO BUSY! I'LL COME OUT AGAIN NEXT WEEK.

ACH. THEN NOW WE MUST DO IT. I'LL—UNNF

GREAT- HAVE ANOTHER HEART ATTACK! LOOK, YOU'LL JUST HAVE TO PAY A BIT MORE FOR HEAT A FEW DAYS LONGER.

GROAN.

I'M -UH- SORRY I MADE YOU TALK SO MUCH, POP.

SO, NEVER MIND, DARLING. ALWAYS IT'S A PLEASURE WHEN YOU VISIT.

The SECOND HONEYMOON

Winter...

WANT SOME COFFEE?

AND SHE SAID: "NO! I WILL NOT GO IN THE GAS CHAMBERS. AND MY *CHILDREN* WILL NOT— CLIK

YOU BET!

Y'KNOW, I'VE GOT OVER 20 HOURS OF VLADEK'S STORY ON TAPE NOW. WE WERE JUST ABOUT *FINISHED* WHEN HE RAN OFF TO FLORIDA.

HE HASN'T CALLED US ONCE. I HOPE HE'S OKAY...

MALA IS DOWN THERE. MAYBE THEY MET AND KILLED EACH OTHER.

ACTUALLY, I THINK THEIR BATTLE KEEPS HIM GOING. HE'S BEEN A BIZARRE COMBINATION OF HELPLESSNESS AND MANIACAL ENERGY EVER SINCE SHE LEFT.

WHAT ARE WE GONNA DO WITH VLADEK? WE SURE AS HELL CAN'T MOVE OUT TO REGO PARK!

MAYBE HE COULD MOVE IN HERE WITH US.

ARE YOU **NUTS**? HIS HEART CAN'T TAKE OUR FOUR FLIGHTS OF STAIRS. IT'S THE BEST THING ABOUT THIS PLACE.

BESIDES, WHAT IF HE SAYS YES!

WELL...IT'S UP TO YOU... HE'S *YOUR* FATHER.

STOP! I FEEL GUILTY ENOUGH ALREADY!

GREAT. THAT SOLVES EVERYTHING!

I WISH HE AND MALA COULD PATCH THINGS UP AND MAKE EACH OTHER MISERABLE AGAIN.

CLIK "AND MY CHILDREN WILL NOT GO IN THE GAS CHAMBERS." SO, TOSHA TOOK THE POISON NOT ONLY TO HERSELF, BUT TO OUR LITTLE

BRING RING!

HELLO. MALA?! WE WERE JUST—HUH? WHAT'S THE MATTER?

I DON'T KNOW IF I'M GOING OR COMING! YOUR FATHER IS IN ST. FRANCIS HOSPITAL.

IT'S THE THIRD TIME IN ONE MONTH—WATER IN THE LUNGS! HE DIDN'T WANT ME TO WORRY YOU, BUT IT'S SERIOUS!

WHEW. WHERE ARE YOU?

IN THE CONDO. SOB. I'M BACK WITH HIM AGAIN, THOUGH GOD KNOWS WHY!

WELL, LOOK. I'LL CALL YOU BACK AFTER I CALL THE HOSPITAL.

HELLO, ST. FRANCIS? CAN I SPEAK TO MR. SPIEGELMAN?...HE'S A PATIENT... WHA?...YOU'RE SURE??

?

HI, MALA? THE HOSPITAL SAYS HE'S NOT REGISTERED THERE.

I KNOW... HE JUST CAME IN THE DOOR!

HE RAN OUT OF THE HOSPITAL AGAINST HIS DOCTOR'S ADVICE. HE SAYS THAT HE DOESN'T TRUST THE DOCTORS HERE.... IT'S CRAZY. HE LOOKS LIKE A GHOST!

HE WANTS TO GO TO HIS N.Y. HOSPITAL. I THINK HE WANTS TO BE NEAR YOU IN CASE, GOD FORBID ANYTHING HAPPENS! I CAN'T HANDLE THIS. COME HELP ME!

GULP.

121

FLORIDA

HEY! EVERYTHING'S AL-MOST *PACKED*, MALA. THE MAIN REASON I FLEW DOWN WAS TO *HELP!*

PSSH. YOU KNOW VLADEK. WILD HORSES CAN'T HOLD HIM STILL... SO NOW HE'S EXHAUSTED, AND ME TOO.

GROAN

HI, POP. HOW ARE YOU?

TERRIBLE. SO WEAK... SO WEAK...

DID YOU ARRANGE EMERGENCY OXY-GEN FOR HIM ON TOMORROW'S PLANE?

UH-HUH. AND I'VE GOT AN AMBULANCE TO TAKE HIM AND ME FROM J.F.K. TO LAGUARDIA HOSPITAL. I'LL CHECK HIM IN WHILE FRANÇOISE DRIVES YOU HOME.

HOW DID YOU TWO GET BACK TOGETHER?

I DON'T KNOW. I GOT A CALL FROM THE HOSPI-TAL AND FELT SORRY FOR HIM. I WENT OVER.

I *SWORE* I'D NEVER SEE HIM AGAIN, BUT I'M JUST A SUCKER. HE TALKED UNTIL I WAS BLUE IN THE FACE... AND HERE I AM.

MALA, MALA! COME QUICK!

ANJA MUST HAVE BEEN A *SAINT!* NO WONDER SHE KILLED HERSELF.

HE'S CALL-ING YOU.

IT'S JUST HIS *STOOL*. HE WANTS ME TO CHECK IT BEFORE HE'LL FLUSH. HE'S AS DIFFICULT AS EVER.

BUT NOW HE'S MORE CON-FUSED AND DEPENDENT. ...WHAT CAN I DO? HE *TRAPPED* ME.

122

Next morning...

AT LAST! WE'RE DONE!

YEAH. ONE HOUR TO PACK, AND *FOUR* HOURS FOR VLADEK TO UNPACK AND REFOLD IT ALL!

I'M *DIZZY* NOW. LET'S GO SIT IN THE FRESH AIR.

YOU GO. I NEED TO CALL MY BROTHER, LEO, AND SAY GOOD-BY BEFORE WE LEAVE.

WHOOSH. A FEW YEARS AGO I WENT OUTSIDE HERE TO BUY FOR MALA BAGELS. I GOT DIZZY, SO LIKE NOW, I GRABBED TO A BUSH, AND I FELL...

I CRAWLED TO THE SIDE SO PEOPLE CAN *SEE* ME BUT WON'T *STEP* ON ME. FINALLY SOMEONE HELPED.

AAH. IT'S GOOD TO GET SOME SUN...

YAH. JUST IT'S TOO NOISY FROM THE HIGHWAY AND AIRPORT NEARBY. *LOOK*, ARTIE! YOU SEE IN THE SKY THAT TINY AIRPLANE?...

UH-HUH.

ON *SUCH* A TINY PLANE WE WENT OUT IN 1946 FROM POLAND TO SWEDEN. IT WAS MAYBE TEN OF US, REFUGEES...

WE NEVER WENT BEFORE IN A PLANE. THE OTHERS WERE *AFRAID* TO GO, BUT I WENT RIGHT AWAY INSIDE...

I SAID TO THEM, "SO DON'T WORRY. *LET* THE PLANE CRASH—AT LEAST WE'LL BE OUT FROM POLAND!"

WHY DID YOU WANT TO LEAVE POLAND?

PSSH. IT WAS **NOTHING** ANYMORE THERE FOR US AFTER THE WAR. NOTHING.

WE WANTED *HERE* TO COME, TO UNCLE HERMAN, BUT HERE WAS **QUOTAS**, SO HERMAN HELPED US TO HAVE A VISA OVER TO STOCKHOLM TO WAIT.

DID YOU WORK THERE?

AND **HOW** I WORKED-HARD LABORS...

I LIFTED AND CARRIED ALL DAY HEAVY BOXES. ONLY **SUCH** JOBS IT WAS FOR REFUGEES.

BUT I WAS **STRONG** THEN NOT SO LIKE NOW... AND I LOOKED TO GET IN A **BETTER** BUSINESS.

ONE DEPARTMENT STORE THERE, A JEW OWNED IT. I WENT TO HIM'...

I'VE BEEN TRYING TO SEE YOU FOR *WEEKS!*

BUT MR. SPIEGELMAN— WE DON'T *NEED* ANY-MORE SALESMEN!...

BESIDES, YOU CAN HARDLY SPEAK SWEDISH!

IN YIDDISH WE SPOKE.

I SOLD TEXTILES AND HOSIERY IN POLAND, BUT I CAN SELL *ANYTHING!*

GIVE ME SOMETHING *NO ONE* CAN SELL—I JUST NEED A **CHANCE!**

HOSIERY? HMM...WE'RE STUCK WITH A WAREHOUSE FULL OF UNFASHIONABLE KNEE-LENGTH STOCKINGS, BUT *NOBODY—*

PERFECT!

IN THE U.S., UNCLE HERMAN AGAIN HAD A HOSIERY FACTORY. BY HIM I GOT FULL-LENGTH **NYLON** STOCKINGS.

THESE IT WAS **IMPOSSIBLE** TO FIND IN SWEDEN.

YOU WANT MY **NYLONS** TO BUY?

DO I?! MY CUSTOMERS WILL **KILL** FOR THESE. THEY'RE RATIONED!

HOW MUCH?

NORMAL PRICE. BUT TO EACH PAIR YOU MUST TAKE ALSO A PAIR OF MY **KNEE**-LENGTHS.

I'LL THROW THEM AWAY, BUT IT'S **WORTH** IT!

AND I SOLD OUT THE WHOLE INVENTORY.

I BECAME SO, LIKE A **PARTNER** TO THIS DEPARTMENT STORE AND **VERY WELL-OFF.**

WHEN IT CAME A FEW YEARS LATER OUR VISAS TO AMERICA, THE STORE MADE A BIG SURPRISE PARTY.

YOU CAN **STILL** RIP UP YOUR BOAT TICKETS AND STAY!

BON VOYAGE

REALLY I WAS SORRY TO GO.

I **MADE** IN THE STATES A LIVING DEALING DIAMONDS, BUT NEVER I HAD IT AGAIN SO GOOD.

SIGH. COME, WE'LL GO NOW INSIDE.

HUH? WHY? WE'VE GOT LOTS OF TIME.

IT'S TOO **SUNNY.** MAYBE IF YOU DIDN'T PACK AWAY MY **SUNGLASSES,** WE COULD **STILL** SIT.

125

Late that night...

PLEASE REMAIN SEATED UNTIL OUR SICK PASSENGER HAS DE-PLANED...

GROAN

J.F.K.

SO THERE WAS A 6 HOUR DELAY BEFORE BOARDING. *THEN* VLADEK COMPLAINS THAT THE OXYGEN UNIT ISN'T WORKING AND HE CAN'T BREATHE.

THE CREW CHECKS AND SAYS THE UNIT IS FINE...

THEY SAY HE'S TOO SICK TO FLY, BUT WE REFUSE TO GET OFF. THEN VLADEK SAYS THE OXYGEN TANK *IS* WORKING, AND HERE WE ARE!

I'M GLAD YOU CALLED TO SAY YOU'D BE LATE.

THEY SET UP A FREE PHONE FOR DELAYED PASSENGERS. MALA CALLED EVERYONE SHE KNOWS IN AMERICA.

YOU SEE? I *LEARNED* FROM VLADEK!

A half hour later...

FINALLY! FRANÇOISE AND MALA MUST BE HOME AND DRY BY NOW. THEY COULD'VE DRIVEN US TO THE HOSPITAL.

DON'T WORRY, THE RIDE IS PAID BY MY *INSURANCE*.

EXCUSE ME. HE'S SICK, BUT I DON'T THINK HE NEEDS A STRETCHER.

REGULATIONS BUDDY.

SO, WHERE *IS* LA GUARDIA HOSPITAL?

ACH! GO ON QUEENS BOULEVARD 'TIL I SAY YOU TO TURN RIGHT.

THANKS, MISTER... BUT *PLEASE* STAY ON THE STRETCHER.

LaGuardia Hospital...

YAWN. WILL IT BE MUCH LONGER?

THE TESTS ARE DONE... YOU CAN WAIT FOR THE DOCTOR IN THERE, WITH YOUR FATHER.

HOW'RE YOU DOIN', POP?

MOAN
SO TIRED...
SO TIRED...

SORRY IT TOOK SO LONG, BUT BECAUSE OF WHAT YOU TOLD US ABOUT YOUR FATHER'S CONDITION, WE PLAYED IT SAFE AND RAN EXTENSIVE TESTS...

THE PILLS HE GOT IN FLORIDA ARE TAKING CARE OF THE WATER IN HIS LUNGS AND HIS HEART SEEMS TO BE DOING FINE...

YOU'LL BE GLAD TO KNOW YOU CAN TAKE HIM HOME WITH YOU!

WHAT?!

UM. IF HE'S A BORDER-LINE CASE, WHY NOT KEEP HIM UNDER OBSER-VATION FOR A FEW DAYS.

THERE'S JUST NO *NEED* FOR HIM TO BE HOSPITALIZED.

WELL, THE DOC-TOR SAYS YOU'RE OKAY. WE CAN GO HOME NOW.

YAH? THEN MALA AND I CAN STAY THE REST OF THE YEAR HERE IN REGO PARK.

IT'S BETTER IF NOTHING IS WRONG *HERE*, NEAR TO MY HEALTH PLAN HOSPITAL, THAN IN A *FLORIDA* HOSPI-TAL FOR HUNDREDS OF DOLLARS A DAY!

A month or so later...

ARTIE, WE HAVEN'T SEEN YOU IN AGES.

I NEEDED TIME TO GET OVER OUR TRIP FROM FLORIDA... WHAT'S NEW?

WELL, WE'RE GOING TO SELL THIS HOUSE AND MOVE DOWN THERE.

I'M AMAZED VLADEK AGREED. HE'S SO ATTACHED TO THIS PLACE.

HOW'S HE FEELING?

HE'S BEEN KIND OF LISTLESS. IT MAKES HIM EASIER TO TAKE, BUT HE'S NOT REALLY DOING TOO WELL.

HE GETS CONFUSED. LAST WEEK HE WENT TO HIS BANK AND ACTUALLY GOT LOST ON THE WAY HOME! ... ANYWAY, HE'S IN THERE RESTING.

SO, I HEAR YOU WANNA SELL THE HOUSE...

YAH? I WANT ONLY PEACE. IF MALA WANTS FLORIDA, OKAY, LET IT BE FLORIDA.

COME AND SIT. I'M SURPRISED TO SEE YOU!

HUH? WHY? I SAID I WAS COMING WHEN I PHONED YOU YESTERDAY.

YOU PHONED? I DON'T REMEMBER...

I CAME TO TAPE THE REST OF YOUR STORY, IF YOU FEEL UP TO IT.

I NEED TO KNOW WHAT HAPPENED AT THE VERY END OF THE WAR...

THE WAR. YAH, THIS I STILL REMEMBER.

YOU WERE LIVING ON A FARM WITH SOME G.I.s...

YAH. WITH MY FRIEND, SHIVEK.

SO, WHAT HAPPENED?

MANY REFUGEES STARTED TO BE EVERYWHERE...

SO, IT CAME AN ORDER...

HEADQUARTERS IS SETTING UP A DISPLACED PERSONS' CAMP. YOU'LL HAVE TO MOVE THERE.

WE ALL CAME OVER TO GARMISCH-PARTENKIRCHEN.

NAME?

VLADEK SPIEGELMAN.

COUNTRY OF ORIGIN?

POLAND...

HERE WE GOT IDENTITY PAPERS AND A PLACE WHERE TO STAY...

HEY, VLADEK. COME WITH ME TO HANNOVER TO SEE MY BROTHER. HE'S MARRIED TO A GENTILE WHO KEPT HIM HIDDEN. HE—

OW!

WHAT'S WRONG?

I DON'T KNOW, SHIVEK. I'VE GOT A FEVER, AND I'M ITCHING ALL OVER—IN MY THROAT, MY EARS, EVERYWHERE! AII!

I WAS FOR A GOOD FEW DAYS VERY SICK.

WH-WHERE AM I?

THE INFIRMARY. YOU'VE HAD A RELAPSE OF TYPHUS.

I FEEL FINE NOW.

SEE A DOCTOR REGULARLY. WE CAN'T DIAGNOSE IT, BUT SOMETHING IS STILL WRONG.

A YEAR AFTER, I FOUND OUT IT WAS NOT ONLY TYPHUS, BUT ALSO DIABETES.

IN THIS DP CAMP, I HAD IT EASY...

HURRY, VLADEK! WE CAN EARN SOME CHOCOLATES!

OKAY! WE SPEAK ENGLISH! OKAY!!

SHIVEK, HE COULDN'T SPEAK EVEN **POLISH**—JUST YIDDISH.

WE CARRIED MANY GOODIES WHEN FINALLY WE GOT OUR I.D. PAPERS TO GO.

WE WANT TICK-ETS TO HANNOVER.

TICKETS??...

I DON'T KNOW IF THERE ARE EVEN ANY *TRACKS!* THAT *FREIGHT* MAY BE HEADING NORTH.

TRAINS STOPPED AND STARTED AND HAD TO CHANGE OFTEN DIRECTIONS...

LOOK, SHIVEK—NUREMBERG.

I SCRUBBED STREETS HERE AS A P.O.W...

NOW IT WAS ONLY STONES AND NOTHING.

WE CAME TO ONE PLACE, WÜRZBURG—WHAT A MESS!

WHERE CAN WE FIND WATER?

HAH! WE HAVEN'T HAD ANY WATER IN THREE DAYS!

THE AMERICANS DESTROYED—SOB—EVERYTHING!

NOT ONE BUILDING WAS STILL STANDING.

WE CAME AWAY HAPPY.

LET THE GERMANS HAVE A *LITTLE* WHAT THEY DID TO THE JEWS.

WE ARRIVED FINALLY TO HANNOVER...

THE KIDS CAN SHARE ONE BEDROOM. YOU TWO CAN HAVE THE OTHER ...

DO YOU KNOW WHERE ANY OF **YOUR** FAMILY IS?

I'LL GO TO POLAND TO SEE IF ANYONE'S LEFT. WE PLANNED TO MEET IN SOSNOWIEC IF WE GOT SEPARATED.

I SENT A LETTER TO THE JEWISH COMMUNITY CENTER THERE, FOR MY WIFE, BUT- SHE CAN'T STILL BE ALIVE... I SAW HER IN AUSCHWITZ LAST YEAR...

SHE WAS SO THIN... SO WEAK...

YOU MIGHT GET NEWS ABOUT YOUR FAMILY AT THE BIG DP CAMP AT BELSEN. JEWS ARE FLOODING IN FROM ALL OVER.

IT WASN'T FAR, SO I WENT FOR A FEW DAYS TO BELSEN. ONE MORNING A CROWD ARRIVED IN, WITH TWO GIRLS WHAT I KNEW A LITTLE FROM MY HOME TOWN ...

JENNY! SONIA!

LOOK! IT'S VLADEK SPIEGELMAN!

WE JUST CAME FROM POLAND...

WE WERE LUCKY TO GET OUT!...

WHATEVER YOU DO, DON'T GO BACK TO SOSNOWIEC. THE POLES ARE STILL KILLING JEWS THERE!

REMEMBER THE GELBERS? THEY OWNED THE BIG BAKERY IN SOSNOWIEC...

"ONE OF THE SONS SURVIVED AND CAME BACK HOME...

WHAT DO **YOU** WANT?

THIS IS MY FAMILY'S HOUSE. I'M GELBER!

WE THOUGHT HITLER FINISHED YOU OFF!

GO AWAY, JEW! THIS IS **OUR** BAKERY NOW!

SLAM!

"HE DIDN'T KNOW WHAT TO DO. HE SPENT THE NIGHT IN THE SHED BEHIND HIS HOUSE...

"THE POLES WENT IN. THEY BEAT HIM AND HANGED HIM.

"...FOR **THIS** HE SURVIVED."

HIS BROTHER CAME FROM THE CAMPS A DAY LATER, AND ONLY STAYED LONG ENOUGH TO BURY HIM...

STOP IT!..I DON'T WANT TO HEAR ANY MORE!

JUST TELL ME. DID YOU HEAR ANYTHING ABOUT ANJA?

I SAW HER! SHE DIDN'T TRY TO GET HER PROPERTY BACK. THE POLES LEAVE HER ALONE.

ANJA IS ALIVE! MY HEART JUMPED! I COULDN'T BELIEVE.

SORRY ANJA. NO NEWS FOR YOU...

EACH DAY SHE CHECKED TO THE JEWISH ORGANIZATION, AND EACH DAY SHE CRIED.

SHE TOLD ME LATER, SHE WENT ONCE TO A GYPSY...

FORTUNES

ANJA KNEW IT WAS FOOLISH, BUT LOOKED ONLY FOR SOME HOPE.

I SEE TRAGEDY...DEATH!... YOU'VE LOST YOUR FATHER... YOUR MOTHER...EVERYONE!

Y-YES. ONLY LOLEK, MY NEPHEW, CAME BACK—

I SEE A CHILD... A DEAD CHILD...

RICHIEU! MY LITTLE BOY, RICHIEU. SOB.

WAIT! NOW I SEE A MAN... ILLNESS...IT'S YOUR HUSBAND! HE'S BEEN VERY, VERY ILL...

HE'S COMING - HE'S COMING HOME! YOU'LL GET A SIGN THAT HE'S ALIVE BY THE TIME THE MOON IS FULL!

I SEE A SHIP...A FARAWAY PLACE... YOU'LL HAVE A NEW LIFE... AND ANOTHER LITTLE BOY.

ANJA WENT A FEW TIMES EACH DAY OVER TO THE JEWISH ORGANIZATION...

BUT NO SIGN CAME OF ME.

SO SHE SAT HOME EVEN MORE DEPRESSED, UNTIL...

KNOCK KNOCK

ANJA! GUESS WHAT! A LETTER FROM YOUR HUSBAND JUST CAME!

HE'S IN GERMANY... HE'S HAD *TYPHUS!*

IT'S JUST LIKE THE GYPSY SAID.

AND HERE'S A *PICTURE* OF HIM! MY GOD-VLADEK IS REALLY ALIVE!

I PASSED ONCE A PHOTO PLACE WHAT HAD A *CAMP* UNIFORM - A NEW AND CLEAN ONE - TO MAKE SOUVENIR PHOTOS...

ANJA KEPT THIS PICTURE ALWAYS. I HAVE IT STILL *NOW* IN MY DESK!

HUH? WHERE DO YOU GO?

I NEED THAT PHOTO IN MY BOOK!

134

INCRED-IBLE!

YAH. SO, WHEN I HEARD ANJA IS *ALIVE* I STOPPED EVERYTHING TO GO ONLY BACK TO SOSNOWIEC.

I TRADED MY THINGS TO HAVE GIFTS.

LOOK! I GOT SOME DRESSES AND A FUR COAT TO BRING ANJA.

Y'KNOW, IF *YOU* GO TO POLAND, I'LL GO TOO!

WE WENT, SOMETIMES BY FOOT, SOMETIMES BY TRAIN.

TO POLAND, MANY TIMES IT WASN'T ANY *TRACKS* LEFT.

ONE PLACE WE STOPPED, HOURS, HOURS AND HOURS.

STAY HERE WITH OUR LUGGAGE, SHIVEK. I'LL GO FILL OUR CANTEENS.

I MARKED OUR TRAIN CAR, BUT WHEN I CAME IN AN HOUR BACK, IT WAS GONE TO ANOTHER TRACK.

SHIVEK?!

I COULDN'T FIND MORE MY FRIEND AND MY LUGGAGE. I HAD ONLY MY THIN SHIRT AND MY WATER.

SHIVEK WENT BACK TO HAN-NOVER TO FIND ME AGAIN...

...BUT I WENT ONLY STRAIGHT TO POLAND. IT TOOK 3 OR 4 WEEKS.

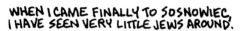

WHEN I CAME FINALLY TO SOSNOWIEC, I HAVE SEEN VERY LITTLE JEWS AROUND.

THERE IT WAS PEOPLE WHAT KNEW ME.

BUT I FOUND OUT WHERE IS THE JEWISH ORGANIZATION.

LOOK WHO'S HERE! SOMEBODY FIND ANJA AND BRING HER RIGHT AWAY!

AND SOMEBODY FOUND HER...

GASP.

V-VLADEK!

IT WAS SUCH A MOMENT THAT EVERYBODY AROUND WAS CRYING TOGETHER WITH US.

ANJA, ANJA, MY ANJA!

MORE I DON'T NEED TO TELL YOU. WE WERE BOTH VERY HAPPY, AND LIVED HAPPY, HAPPY EVER AFTER.

SO... LET'S STOP, PLEASE, YOUR TAPE RECORDER...

I'M *TIRED* FROM TALKING, RICHIEU, AND IT'S *ENOUGH* STORIES FOR NOW...

SPIEGELMAN

VLADEK
Oct. 11, 1906
Aug 18, 1982

ANJA
Mar. 15, 1912
May 21, 1968

— art spiegelman — 1978-1991